Praise for *Everest: Mountain Without Mercy:*

"It's a great picture book. For anyone with the remotest
interest in the story of the mountain."
—*New York Times Book Review*

"If any book captures the majesty and sheer power
of the world's most awe-inspiring mountain, this is it."
—*Copley News Service*

"As breathtakingly beautiful and grueling as the mountain itself."
—*Providence Sunday Journal*

"Packed with breathtaking images."
—*People*

"*Everest* describes the making of what must surely be one of the most
challenging films ever attempted. But it also tells a story of suffering,
loss, and courage. When lives hung in the balance, David Breashears and
Ed Viesturs put the camera down and performed heroically."
—Jon Krakauer, author of *Into Thin Air*

Praise for the MacGillivray Freeman IMAX film *Everest*:

"Not only a visually glorious and absorbing film and a story
of hope and hubris; it is also an amazing feat of filmmaking."
—*New York Times*

"As close as you can get without doing it yourself."
—*Boston Herald*

"Captures both the majesty of the mountain
and the madness of those who seek to conquer it."
—*Boston Globe*

"A breathtaking climb to the top of Mount Everest that reveals the
world's highest mountain in all of its awesome, perilous grandeur."
—*Entertainment Weekly*

EVEREST
Mountain Without Mercy

BROUGHTON COBURN
FOREWORD BY CONRAD ANKER

NATIONAL GEOGRAPHIC

WASHINGTON, D.C.

*For the Venerable Ngawang Tenzing Jangpo,
the Incarnate Lama of the Tengboche Monastery*

In 1996, MacGillivray Freeman Films filmed an amazing story that
unfolded on the tallest mountain on Earth. In May of that year,
Mount Everest claimed the lives of 15 climbers in its deadliest season ever.
The resulting IMAX film, *Everest,* became the highest grossing
documentary film of all time, surpassing $152 million at the box office.
In response to the film's overwhelming international success, MacGillivray
Freeman Films returned to the mountain in 2007 to document the largest ever
study of hypoxia. Forty doctors and 200 patients turned Everest into the highest
medical laboratory ever conceived. The upcoming film based on that
challenging and heroic effort, *Return to Everest,* will be released in 2017.
Audiences can still experience *Everest* in select IMAX theaters,
by streaming online, or on DVD.

✳ ✳ ✳

In this updated edition of *Everest: Mountain Without Mercy,* we have
kept the core story of the film expedition, the tragedies, and the rescues.
We have illustrated it both with photographs taken during the expedition—
signaled by "1996" at the beginning of a caption—and with pictures
taken before and since. We have added a feature called Flash Forward that gives
a glimpse of what has happened to many of the main characters in the drama since 1996.
We have updated maps and statistics to the best of our ability as of May 2015,
when the full impact of the April 2015 earthquake and avalanche was still unknown.

(previous spread) 1996: Often capped by cloud, Everest makes its own weather while it
lures adventurers with the ultimate challenge. Though more climbers are summiting than
ever before, Everest remains a dangerous enterprise. *(opposite)* From the air, Mount Everest
and the Khumbu Glacier look beautiful, but almost insurmountable.

CONTENTS

THE CHANGING FACE OF EVEREST

BY CONRAD ANKER

What is it that attracts us to Everest? The lack of oxygen and the extreme cold make it inhospitable. The steep, icy slopes give gravity the upper hand. Any mistake is magnified and can result in injury or death. Somehow, in spite of this, there is a draw. Is it as simple as pioneering Everest climber George Mallory's pithy yet rhetorical answer when asked why he climbed: "Because it's there"? Is it the allure of experiencing nature in its most raw and unbridled form?

Or is it the ego, which motivates so many human actions? Perhaps it is a combination of all these things. Standing on the summit confirms a sense of ruggedness, perseverance, and skill—attributes that would make any person proud.

Regardless of the motivation, climbing Everest is a quest that many have dreamed of but relatively few have undertaken. Climbing Everest has become symbolic of human achievement, ever since the first recorded summit in 1953. As much as that goal stands fixed and permanent in the world's imagination, the forces of plate tectonics mean that Everest continues to grow taller regardless of our presence on its slopes. In the six-plus decades since it was first climbed, it is estimated to have risen just over 12 centimeters. Though it's gotten higher since Sir

1996: **Aglow from within, climbers' lantern-illuminated tents nestle at Everest Base Camp.**

Conrad Anker descends through the Khumbu Icefall: a treacherous sea of ice that every summit hopeful has to navigate.

Edmund Hillary and Tenzing Norgay's summit in 1953, in many ways the peak has become easier to climb. On the standard routes, both from Nepal and Tibet, ropes guide climbers from the mountain's base to the summit. Affixed to the ropes are ascenders, mechanical clamps that allow secure upward travel. In the 1950s, climbers used rope to stay tethered to each other as they ventured into the unexplored. Today, fixed ropes allow climbers and Sherpa guides to move more freely and provide an escape hatch in case of bad weather or accidents. What was once unexplored is now a sidewalk stamped into condition. Climbers acclimatize in camps built decades before, their platforms carved into the mountainside. Oxygen systems are more

efficient today, delivering the element most vital to human survival at half the weight the 1950s teams had to carry. The use of supplemental oxygen has become a choice rather than a necessity. If reaching the summit is the priority, the question has become: How much oxygen can a climber afford? Climbers with means can hire Sherpas to lug expensive bottles of gas up the mountain for them. Life at Base Camp features heated tents, fresh food, and real-time communications, which all bring the experience much closer to civilization. The Nepali staff make the present-day Everest experience almost comfortable. From the porters to the cooks to the high-altitude guides, modern Everest expeditions rest on the shoulders of the people employed to help climbers realize their dreams. Everest has risen, and our hopes and ambitions have continued to rise along with it.

Yet big dreams and small comforts can't stop Everest from being a dangerous place. Tragedy has struck expeditions on Everest for as long as people have been climbing it. In 1922, seven Sherpas lost their lives in an avalanche. The same dynamic took place 92 years later on April 18, 2014, when a massive ice avalanche killed 17 Nepali climbers. The Sherpas killed in this accident were all working for visiting climbers, carrying their equipment up through the treacherous Khumbu Icefall. In truth, the risks of climbing Everest haven't gone away: Climbers have increasingly transferred those risks onto the Sherpas instead of themselves. The 2014 tragedy brought the world's attention to the personal and cultural costs associated with high-altitude Himalayan climbing—the same costs that came into sharp relief on May 10 and 11, 1996.

When MacGillivray Freeman Films sent an IMAX film team to Everest in 1996, the mountain was in full-swing transition from nation-based expeditions to commercial guiding. Where before teams were fueled by patriotic ambition, now they were motivated by ego: supported by personal, corporate, and philanthropic backing, all wanting to stand on top of the world. Smaller, multinational teams—professional, organized, and with extensive Sherpa support—were becoming the norm.

The first news of the 1996 Everest tragedies reached me on my morning commute on a rainy spring day in Oakland, California. The staid reporter for National Public Radio announced the effects of a sudden storm on the southeast buttress of Everest. In one day, eight climbers lost their lives. It was the deadliest single day in Everest history. For me, it was a haunting moment. Several of the guides and clients were my friends and peers in the international climbing community. Rob Hall and I had guided together in Antarctica; Scott Fischer was a man whom I looked up to.

As the day unfolded, I learned more about the storm that had unexpectedly slammed into the Everest massif. In 1996, weather forecasting was general and based on the success of the previous season. We have since replaced luck with more refined and accurate forecasts for wind and precipitation, but by all accounts May 11 was an auspicious day. The attention-grabbing headlines changed the way the public viewed the planet's highest peak. They made it clear that the bar for entry on Everest, once set by climbing experience, was now determined by the depth of one's bank account. This notable season also established the now annual attention that fixes on Everest each May.

> " **The mountain decides whether you climb** or not. The art of mountaineering is knowing when to go, when to stay, and when to retreat. "
>
> ~ED VIESTURS,
> AMERICAN CLIMBER

Looking up at the Khumbu Glacier, Anker reflects. Despite the dangers Everest poses, climbers continue to feel drawn to the mountain.

After 1996, we thought fewer people would want to climb the mountain. Instead of keeping inexperienced climbers at bay, the disaster seemed to draw them toward Everest in ever growing numbers.

The 1996 season prompted heart-wrenching sadness and complex questions about commercialization and crowding on Everest. But did it change the way we climb the mountain, both physically and emotionally?

The helicopter-assisted ascent in 2014 is an example of how climbing has changed on Everest. The Nepali climbing community voluntarily ended the season after the April 18th avalanche, but one climber chose to pursue the summit, flying over the Icefall and striking for the summit with a team of top-drawer climbing Sherpas. While an isolated incident, it is a testament to how, for some, the prize—summiting Everest—may now be reached without the journey. This new development forever changes the nature of the game.

Everest will continue to be pushed higher into the troposphere, and if history is anything to go on, our interest will follow. Our fascination with the human condition at 29,000 feet is not going to fade away, even in the face of tragedy. We want to understand why humans are driven to endure a degree of suffering and risk that may cost them their lives. Some things have changed on Everest, but the fundamental story remains the same: It has always been about the desire to challenge the unknown. About how facing uncertainty at -40°F without oxygen, standing at the edge of our capability, allows us a glimpse into our own souls. That is why *Everest: Mountain Without Mercy*—and the award-winning IMAX film that inspired it—is as relevant today as it was when it was first published in 1997. As you read through these pages you might ask yourself, "What would it be like to be caught on that mountain? What would I do if I was?"

An icy highway to Everest's lower reaches: the Western Cwm dwarfs climbers bound for Camp II.

CLIMBING EVEREST

■ Milestones
■ Disasters

LANDMARKS IN THE MOUNTAIN'S HISTORY 1921–2014

»1922: First Summit Attempt
Another British expedition, including George Mallory, returns to make an attempt on the mountain. An avalanche sweeps nine porters into a crevasse. Though two are found alive, these become the first reported deaths on Everest.

»1950: One Side Opens, Another Closes Nepal opens its borders, making it easier for ambitious climbers to attempt climbing Everest, while the northern approach used by previous expeditions is closed to Westerners.

»1960: Climbing the North Face A Chinese expedition claims a first ascent of the mountain's north side, but a lack of evidence casts doubt over their supposed victory.

»1970: A Crowded Season
An avalanche kills six Sherpas. It is the worst tragedy for the Sherpa community since 1922, highlighting the danger of the Khumbu Icefall.

»1970: Skiing Down Everest
Yuichiro Miura skis from the South Col. A 1975 documentary about his adventure becomes the first sports film to win an Academy Award for Best Documentary Feature.

»1975: A Woman Ascends
Japanese climber Junko Tabei becomes the first woman to reach the summit.

»1975: Mounting the Southwest Face A British team led by Chris Bonington climbs the Southwest Face.

R. Messner

»1980: A Winter Ascent
Polish climbers Leszek Cichy and Krzysztof Wielicki become the first to summit Everest, or any 8,000-meter peak, in winter.

»1980: Going Solo
Superclimber Reinhold Messner makes the first solo ascent of Everest, again without supplementary oxygen.

»1980: Climbing the North Face Takashi Ozaki and Tsuneo Shigehiro become the first to make a full ascent of the North Face.

»1953: A Successful Summit
As part of the ninth British expedition to Everest, Edmund Hillary and Tenzing Norgay climb the South Face of Everest to become the first people to stand on the summit.

»1974: A Major Incident
On an expedition led by Frenchman Gérard Devouassoux, bad weather causes an avalanche, burying six climbers. It is the worst single incident yet recorded.

»1978: Everest Without Oxygen
Reinhold Messner and Peter Habeler become the first to summit the mountain without using supplementary oxygen.

»1924: Mystery of Mallory and Irvine
Mallory and Irvine disappear above 26,700 feet. Noel Odell says he thought he saw them near the top, but can't prove they summited.

Early climbing gear

»1963: First American to Summit
Jim Whittaker becomes the first American to reach the summit, accompanied by Nawang Gombu, who later becomes the first person to climb Everest twice.

»1963: Traversing the Mountain
Americans Tom Hornbein and Willi Unsoeld pioneer the West Ridge route and descend by the South Col, making the mountain's first traverse.

»1921: Reconnaissance Mission
Guy Bullock and George Mallory of Great Britain become the first climbers to reach the North Col, establishing the northern route up Mount Everest.

Americans on top

12

>> **2000: Speeding up the Mountain** Babu Chiri Sherpa climbs from Base Camp to the summit in under 17 hours, establishing a new South Face speed-ascent record.

>> **2007: Rising Crowds** The mountain sees a record 633 successful summits, highlighting long-held concerns about overcrowding, inexperience, and commercialization on Everest.

Climbing the Kangshung

>> **1983: Climbing the Kangshung Face** American Lou Reichardt and his teammates make the first ascent of the Kangshung (East) Face.

>> **1995: The Last Frontier** Japanese climbers Kiyoshi Furuno and Shigeki Imoto are the first climbers to summit the last remaining unclimbed route, along the full Northeast Ridge.

>> **1998: Overcoming Adversity** Tom Whittaker, whose right foot had been amputated, becomes the first disabled person to successfully reach the summit.

Waiting in line

>> **2012: Tragic Traffic Jam** Ten people die in the course of the season. Four deaths are blamed on a traffic jam that forces tired climbers to wait in line as they attempt to descend.

>> **2015: Earthquake and Aftermath** On April 25, a 7.9-magnitude earthquake causes a major avalanche that devastates Base Camp and leaves climbers stranded at higher camps. The avalanche kills at least 18 people and injures more than 60, making it the deadliest single day in Everest history.

>> **1996: A Deadly Season** Eight climbers die in a storm, including guides Rob Hall and Scott Fischer. Fifteen perish in the course of the season, making it the deadliest yet.

>> **2011: Record Number of Ascents** Apa Sherpa claims the most successful summits of all time: 21 in total.

Summiting late in 1996

>> **1988: Paragliding Down** Jean-Marc Boivin climbs the Southeast Ridge, then puts on a portable paraglider and makes an 11-minute flight to Camp II.

>> **1982: Lost in the Pinnacles** Peter Boardman and Joe Tasker disappear between the First and Second Pinnacles, which had yet to be climbed, on the Northeast Ridge.

>> **1982: A Hard Climb** A Soviet expedition climbs a route on the Southwest Face, which comes to be known as the hardest route yet climbed.

>> **2006: Left for Dead** A solo climber named David Sharp is found comatose on the mountain and dies soon after. No one had reported him missing, even though he was passed by over 40 climbers. Days later, Australian Lincoln Hall is left for dead, only to be found alive the next day. Both events spark huge controversy about accountability on Everest.

>> **1999: Finding Mallory** Conrad Anker, a member of an American research expedition, discovers the body of George Mallory at 26,700 feet on the North Face.

>> **2014: Death on the Icefall** Seventeen Sherpas die in an avalanche on the Khumbu Icefall, prompting outrage over the low insurance rates and financial assurances for climbing Sherpas and their families.

Lighting candles for the dead

PROLOGUE

On the morning of May 10, the steep, knife-edge ridge connecting the South Summit of Mount Everest to the Hillary Step was clearly visible from Camp II, 7,300 vertical feet below. High clouds raced past the summit, and high winds scoured the Southeast Ridge, emitting a distant, ominous roar. In the early afternoon, David Breashears and Ed Viesturs trained their binoculars on the South Summit and spotted six or seven climbers traversing the ridge.

Directly ahead, several more climbers were waiting at the base of the Hillary Step, an awkward and craggy stretch of 40 vertical feet of rock and snow leading to the summit that can only be managed one climber at a time. David and Ed would later learn that the ropes needed to assist climbers had been fixed on the Step later in the morning than guides Rob Hall and Scott Fischer had planned.

Even when fixed promptly, a time-consuming bottleneck can occur when too many climbers arrive at the Step at the same time.

Squinting into a telescope, David and Ed calculated the climbers' rate of ascent and their use of bottled oxygen: Their oxygen might last through the summit attempt, and the weather was fair. Nevertheless, Ed's face worked with concern. It was very

1996: **Delays on May 10 force climbers to wait just below the treacherous Hillary Step.**

The 2012 National Geographic expedition team navigates through early morning darkness on the dangerous Khumbu Icefall.

late in the day for climbers to be attempting to summit. Because it can take 18 hours to make the round-trip from Camp IV to the top of Everest under the best of conditions, almost all climbers try to summit before midday. The climbers Ed and David observed would almost certainly be descending in the fading light of late afternoon—a potentially dangerous situation.

"They've already been climbing 14 hours, and they *still* aren't on the summit. Why haven't they turned around?" Ed asked David. There was no answer. Ed was glad of one thing: that he wasn't waiting in line with them.

Ed and Paula Viesturs had been on Everest with New Zealander Rob Hall's group the two previous years, and Paula was chatting with Helen Wilton, Hall's manager at the New Zealand Base Camp. They were eager to hear news from the summit, and at about 1:25 p.m. whoops and cheers issued from the dining tent of American Scott Fischer's Mountain Madness group—his guides and clients had just radioed from the top. Fischer himself had said he was having a slow day. He had not reached the

> 66
>
> . . . my compadres dallied to memorialize their arrival at the apex of the planet . . . None of them imagined that **a horrible ordeal** was drawing nigh. Nobody suspected that by the end of that long day, **every minute would matter.**
>
> ~JON KRAKAUER,
> *INTO THIN AIR*
>
> 99

summit yet, but apparently chose to continue climbing slowly rather than help guide his clients down. They passed him as they descended.

Neither Rob Hall nor his clients had made it to the top yet. Around 2:30 Paula and Helen heard Hall's summit radio call. It was windy, he reported; those on his team who had summited were descending, except for client Doug Hansen. He could see Hansen approaching slowly, and had decided to wait for him at the top. Paula was surprised that Rob would summit with a client this late, contrary to his own rule that his team should descend no later than 2 p.m.

Paula was tempted to join in the cheering, but thought it premature. She worried about Hansen, and was well aware of how dangerous and treacherous Everest could be. The year before, Chantal Mauduit had been climbing behind Ed Viesturs when she collapsed at the South Summit while attempting to be the first woman to summit without supplemental oxygen. In an extremely difficult rescue, the Sherpas, Ed, Rob Hall, and two other climbers had to drag and lower her down the summit ridge to Camp IV on the South Col. On that climb Ed had also encountered Hall's client Doug Hansen staggering below the South Summit. Hansen was not clipped in to the fixed rope, and Ed shouted at him to stop. Ed gave Hansen his only oxygen bottle, but Hansen was still having trouble descending even as Guy Cotter, Hansen's guide, assisted him back to the South Col.

"Keep me informed," Paula told Helen, as she returned to her Base Camp kitchen tent to make dinner.

1996: **Rock cairns near Everest Base Camp mark this as a spiritual "power spot."**

CHAPTER ONE

A MOUNTAIN OF A DREAM

"Several seasons of good weather have led people to think of Everest as benevolent," *Everest* Film Expedition leader David Breashears observed. "But in the mid-eighties—before many of the *guides* had been on Everest—there were three consecutive seasons when no one climbed the mountain because of the ferocious wind. Everest can be a place where people can't see or move, where tents are ripped apart, where all the high-tech gear in the world can't save you."

Yet Everest casts a spell, and many remain undeterred. Between 1921 and 1996, more than 169 people died on the mountain—one for every five who reached the summit. Since then, a swell in the number of guided treks up Everest has seen that ratio come closer to one death for every 55 ascents, but nothing assures safety on the world's highest mountain. In the 19 years since 1996, 112 people have died on the mountain. Most of the dead are still there.

Mount Everest hasn't always attracted such misfortune. As far as is known, no one considered climbing Everest until long after the British commissioned the Great Trigonometrical Survey, a monumental effort to survey and measure all of India and the Himalaya. Undertaken in the mid-19th century,

Rosy light flatters Everest and the Khumbu Glacier, luring climbers toward the summit.

the survey identified the world's tallest mountain, assigned it a provisional height, and gave it a name: Mount Everest, in honor of India's previous surveyor general, George Everest.

AN UNUSUAL CONCEPT

Filmmaker Greg MacGillivray, a pioneer of large-format cinematography, had long been fascinated by Everest exploration and mountaineering—the dramatic story of human achievement and heroism set against almost insurmountable odds. He carefully studied climbing films, which he felt were limited in their ability to capture the splendor of the mountains and the spectacle of climbing them. Someone had to be able to do it better, and IMAX was the medium to match the Himalaya. In IMAX theaters, audiences are surrounded by six channels of synchronized digital sound, and scenes are projected at ten times the resolution of a 35-mm feature film on screens that are up to eight stories tall and 100 feet wide.

"Just as the wide screen of Cinema Scope was perfect for the landscapes of John Ford's westerns of the 1950s," Mac-Gillivray said, "the more vertical ratio aspect of IMAX is perfect for Everest."

In June of 1994, MacGillivray contacted David Breashears to ask if he might like to shoot and direct the on-mountain visuals for a film on Everest—and help organize the expedition to the mountain.

Breashears was the obvious choice. A veteran of 18 Himalayan expeditions, he was the first American to summit Everest twice and had already made many films on and around the mountain. He was intrigued by MacGillivray's proposal, but concluded that hauling a full-size IMAX camera to the summit would be impossible.

Always game for a challenge within the realm of safety, however, Breashears figured he'd try to convince MacGillivray to shoot the high-mountain

> "
> We agreed that this was going to be **no ordinary climb.** For the time being, Everest was rather more than a mountain.
>
> ~JOHN HUNT,
> LEADER OF THE
> 1953 EXPEDITION
> "

footage in a more manageable format, such as 35mm. "I'm interested," he responded confidently. Breashears had transmitted the first live television images from Everest's summit 11 years earlier, and knew that a feature movie camera would be only slightly larger than a video camera.

But MacGillivray was firm; the images would have to be shot in IMAX. Smaller formats, he argued, wouldn't work on the big screens of the museum theaters that typically show these large-format films. He could see the logistical problems that transporting the camera posed, but wouldn't lower his expectations. His production company would simply have to build a smaller camera, and then provide the resources and support for an expedition that could make it happen.

Breashears accepted, and he began by providing specifications for a modified IMAX camera. He soon found out what many had learned the hard way: In IMAX, nothing is easy.

"Weight will be one challenge," Breashears said with visible concern. The risks of climbing above 26,000 feet were well documented—and frightening, as he knew from earlier expeditions. He had escorted one blind and exhausted climber down the Southeast Ridge, and had recovered bodies from all over the mountain. Most of these climbers were victims, at least indirectly, of the effects of altitude. On Everest, the margin of safety is extremely small.

Greg MacGillivray wanted to produce a film that would educate as it entertained. To identify and explore the unique issues that relate to Mount Everest, he and Breashears carefully assembled a team of ten academic advisers. These advisers, all longtime observers of the Himalaya, portrayed an unusual and dynamic mountain: Geologists described Everest not

1996: **Barehanded at 21,400 feet, expedition leader David Breashears reloads film with help from Robert Schauer.**

as a static geological monument but as a mountain in motion; meteorologists explained that the Himalaya and its associated plateau are thought to influence much of the world's weather patterns; physiologists observed that Everest's summit is at the very limit of man's ability to survive; and anthropologists portrayed the rich culture of the Sherpa, a resourceful people who have thrived in the shadow of these mountains for more than four centuries.

Over a period of a year, an experienced team was assembled, consisting of four climbers, four filmmakers, two Base Camp support staff, twenty-four Sherpas, and three on-site advisers and journalists—a total of 37 people on the mountain.

TO KATHMANDU

Before 1950, Everest expeditions approached the mountain through Tibet. Nepal's complementary barriers of topography and isolationist policy had effectively insulated it from the rest of the world. But in that year, Nepal began to open its borders to the outside world. For climbers, the gates to a tantalizing, magical, and daunting kingdom had been unlocked. Eight of the world's ten highest mountains are located within Nepal (or on the border with Tibet or Sikkim), and until the 1950s none of them had been climbed.

In early March 1996, the *Everest* film expedition members departed their countries for Kathmandu,

> 66
> By all pragmatic standards **climbing mountains is 'useless.'** That, indeed, is **one of its glories:** that it needs no end or justification beyond itself—like a sunset, a symphony, or like falling in love.
>
> ~JAMES RAMSEY ULLMAN,
> *AMERICANS ON EVEREST*
> 99

Nepal's capital, a scenic destination from any approach.

As a plane begins its descent into the city, half the Nepali Himalaya are visible. From Dhaulagiri to Everest, the world's most imposing peaks rise like an apparition. Mountain slopes graced with snow and forested high valleys beckon seductively. The plane crosses a pass and the city appears, surrounded by corn and rice terraces that are sculpted on the rim of the Kathmandu valley like topographic map contours.

From the taxi window, it is clear that this ancient city is embracing the transition from the 12th century to the 21st. But the pavement and neon seem a temporary and superficial dressing, as if the city's urban cows, wandering sadhus, centuries-old temples, and stone deities will momentarily rise up and sweep aside the trappings of the modern age.

The team members converged at the Yak and Yeti Hotel. "What country is your expedition from?" one hotel guest asked. Spain, Japan, Austria, the U.K., India, Nepal, and the U.S., to start with. Stacked on the reception desk was a colorful pile of dog-eared passports.

CLIMBERS, FILMMAKERS, AND ADVISERS

David Breashears knew that in selecting climbers, experience and compatibility would be critical; the team would be spending at least two and a half months together. He and Greg MacGillivray

---

FLASH FORWARD **ED VIESTURS**

In 2002, Viesturs was awarded the Lowell Thomas Award for his achievements in mountaineering. In 2005, he completed his 18-year Endeavor 8000 project by climbing Annapurna, making him one of the few people (and the only American) to have summited the world's fourteen 8,000-meter peaks and the sixth person to have done so without supplemental oxygen. Named National Geographic's Adventurer of the Year that year, Viesturs went on to write several books about his climbing adventures, including *The Mountain: My Time on Everest.*

wanted an international team as well, and to offer a shot at Everest for expert climbers who might not otherwise have the opportunity.

For deputy leader, MacGillivray and Breashears chose American mountaineer Ed Viesturs, a three-time Everest summiter who was keen to climb it again, his third time without supplemental oxygen.

After graduating from the University of Washington in 1981, Ed attended Washington State University's veterinary school and guided for RMI, a guide service on Mount Rainier. In 12 years, he summited Rainier 187 times. He also climbed Denali and Aconcagua before being invited to Everest in 1987. By 1996, he had embarked on a quest he called Endeavor 8000: to summit the world's 14 highest peaks, those over 8,000 meters (26,250 feet), without supplemental oxygen. He completed that quest in 2005, making him one of only six people to have climbed all of the world's highest peaks without bottled oxygen, and the only American. "This is a personal goal for me," Ed explained. "It's not for fame." Friends have nicknamed him "Steady Ed" for his consistency and professionalism.

"One of the joys of being with Ed is knowing you are in the presence of a superior being," Breashears summarized. "His stamina and reliability are phenomenal."

Ed's wife Paula Viesturs had worked in Base Camp on a previous expedition, and the filmmakers chose her to be Base Camp manager. A hiker and beginning climber, she would provide logistical support while the climbers were on the mountain.

MacGillivray and Breashears next chose Araceli Segarra, of Lleida, Catalonia, whom Breashears had met a year earlier on the north side of Everest. A professional physiotherapist, Araceli is a versatile ice, rock, and alpine climber. She climbed the South Face of Shisha Pangma (26,291 feet) alpine style in

An elated Ed Viesturs takes a self-portrait on Everest's summit.

1992, and in 1995 she attempted the North Face of Everest, reaching 25,591 feet. If successful, she would be the first Catalan—and Spanish—woman to climb Mount Everest.

Araceli came to climbing through spelunking. Having trained for years in Spain's vast limestone cave systems, she brought an abundance of enthusiasm and optimism to the team. "Mainly, I like to climb with friends and to enjoy, especially when there's a nice route. When I climb a rock wall I dance and connect movements without thinking or breathing the words 'I'm falling, I'm falling.' And with friends—there is nothing better."

Climbing leader Jamling Tenzing Norgay, of Darjiling, West Bengal, India, is an experienced

(Continued on page 26)

mountaineer and expedition organizer. This would be his first Everest attempt. His father, Tenzing Norgay, reached the summit of Mount Everest with Sir Edmund Hillary on the historic first ascent in 1953. A devout Buddhist like his father, Jamling deeply respects the deities that reside on and around Everest.

"Each year on the anniversary of my father's climb, the 29th of May, at least one member of my family places a silk *kata* blessing scarf on the scroll painting of Miyolangsangma, the goddess of Everest, that we keep on our altar. It was to her that my father expressed gratitude when he reached the summit.

"I'm hoping that the culture of the Sherpas will be viewed more widely as a result of the film of this expedition," he added.

(previous spread) From the air, the Himalaya range reveals the immensity of its sharp peaks and deep valleys.

In 1975, Junko Tabei was the first woman to summit Everest—by1996, no other Japanese woman had yet climbed it. Breashears met Sumiyo Tsuzuki in 1990 on the north side of Everest. She had been on Everest twice before and had climbed to 23,000 feet on Everest's North Col in 1995. Sumiyo would be documenting the expedition on video.

"To go on an expedition and climb you need high concentration, which we do not have in city life," Sumiyo said. "That, I enjoy."

To help muscle around the streamlined IMAX camera—and for an extra head to think in conditions of oxygen starvation—David would need to work with another accomplished climbing cinematographer. Robert Schauer of Graz, Austria, assistant cameraman for the film team, is David's European mirror image. "I had read about Robert when I was younger," Breashears said, "and it's an honor for me to climb

Sir Edmund Hillary (left) and Tenzing Norgay are all smiles after becoming the first people to summit Mount Everest in 1953.

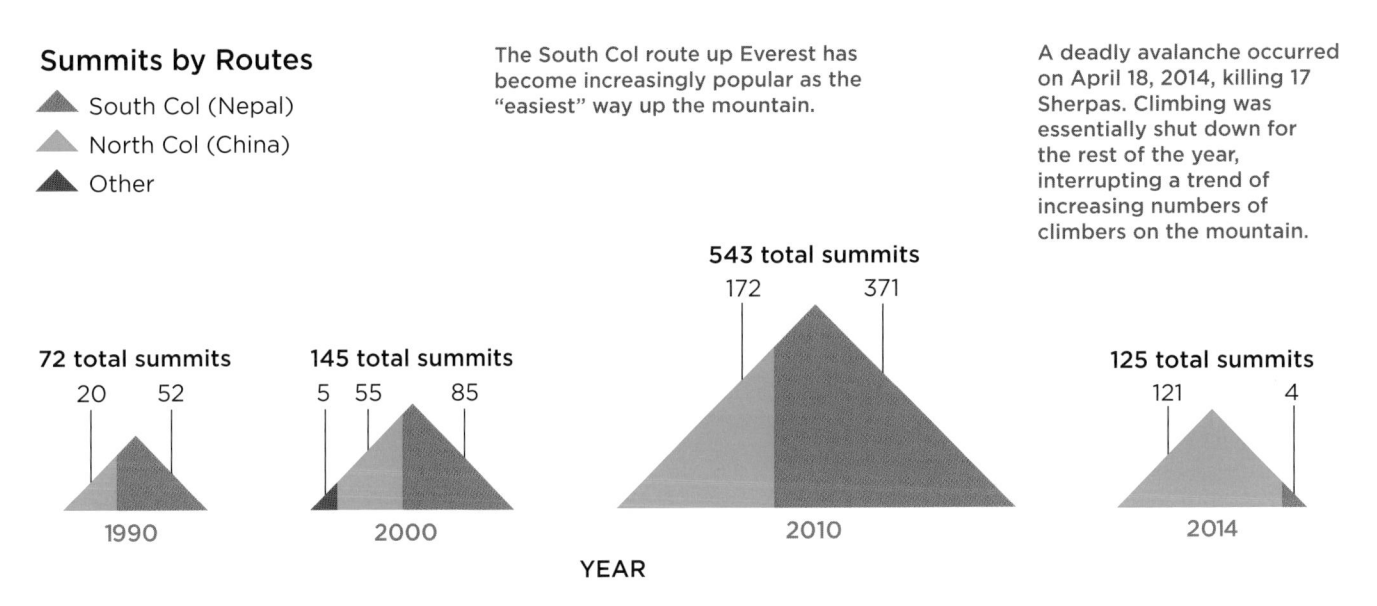

Summits by Routes

▲ South Col (Nepal)
▲ North Col (China)
▲ Other

The South Col route up Everest has become increasingly popular as the "easiest" way up the mountain.

A deadly avalanche occurred on April 18, 2014, killing 17 Sherpas. Climbing was essentially shut down for the rest of the year, interrupting a trend of increasing numbers of climbers on the mountain.

543 total summits
172 · 371

72 total summits
20 · 52

145 total summits
5 · 55 · 85

125 total summits
121 · 4

1990 · 2000 · 2010 · 2014

YEAR

and to film with him." Schauer had produced or co-produced 12 mountain and adventure films and documentaries, and had climbed five of the world's fourteen 8,000-meter peaks. He was the first Austrian to reach Everest's summit, 18 years earlier.

Pleased with the chosen team, Robert noted, "We are already working together well, and our humor and spirit are flowing."

A few days after the climbing and film teams arrived, a seasoned Nepal hand dragged several battered bags into the Yak and Yeti. They belonged to Roger Bilham, a professor of geology at the University of Colorado in Boulder and adviser to the film. Two of the suitcases were filled with tools, transistors, superglue, batteries, a laptop computer, and some heavy wire that looked suspiciously like bent coat hangers.

"Roger knows a great deal about everything," David said proudly. Ed referred to the transplanted British national as "our team geophysicist." Roger had already been working with the government of Nepal on establishing a network of Global Positioning System (GPS) satellite receivers to measure movements of the tectonic plates beneath the Himalaya.

> " It is still there. It always will be. And **it is time we had a look** for ourselves.
>
> ~NORMAN DYHRENFURTH, ABOUT THE 1963 AMERICAN EXPEDITION "

He would be taking GPS readings along the approach route—which partly follows the dynamic junction of the Eurasian and Indian landmasses. He would also oversee the placement of the world's highest weather station, at 26,800 feet on Everest, and take a GPS reading there as well.

Another British national joining the team as correspondent was historian Audrey Salkeld. She had written a book about George Mallory and Sandy Irvine, the Everest explorers who had disappeared in 1924, either en route to the summit or while descending. Though not a climber herself, Audrey had been to the north side of Everest with David Breashears in 1986.

Steve Judson, one of the more experienced writers and directors of large-format IMAX films, had been on numerous shoots, but none quite as remote or logistically difficult as Everest. As co-writer (with Tim Cahill) and editor of the film, Steve would be working with photographic and technical consultant Brad Ohlund, who had 20 years of experience as a second-unit director of photography with MacGillivray Freeman Films.

Steve and Brad would travel to Base Camp. En route, they would help David and Robert develop their large-format cinematography skills. Once the camera went above Base Camp, David and Robert would be on their own.

The team knew that virtually no ascent of Everest had begun without the indigenous people of the Everest region, the Sherpas. Most of the 20 Sherpas hired for the film expedition had flown or hiked to Kathmandu from Khumbu, the valleys that enclose the approach route to Base Camp. They brought with them, as always, their customary good cheer and playful humor.

Wongchu Sherpa, the *sirdar* (head man) in charge of the Sherpas and Nepal logistics, was among the most entertaining members of the team. He seemed to revel in the constant battle with bureaucrats over the frustrating permit process, and over which his joking banter and quick-wittedness usually prevailed.

David and Wongchu were on Everest together in 1986. Wongchu himself had climbed Everest from the north in 1995, and had acted as sirdar for several expeditions. "I now hire the climbing Sherpas who hired me—we joke about this," Wongchu said.

WHY CLIMB?

For climbing Sherpas, climbing is a job, not something they would undertake for sport. Climbing Sherpas can make $1,200 to $5,000 a season, in a country with a per capita income of around $700 a year. But only the top sirdars and those with access to investment money own houses and businesses in the capital—where land prices exceed those of many wealthy American residential communities.

So what motivates the others who come to Everest? "Maybe they have lots of time and money and don't

The first American team to summit Mount Everest, 1963, battled through intense wind, epic ice, and exhaustion.

IMAX ON EVEREST
HEARTBREAK, COURAGE, AND TRIUMPH

I was a world away from our *Everest* film team on May 10, when tragedy struck the mountain. At our production office in Laguna Beach, California, I received a satellite call from Brad Ohlund, our director of photography, stationed at Everest Base Camp. I've worked with Brad on 35 IMAX films and I barely recognized his voice. High elevations wreak havoc on our upper respiratory systems, and Brad had already been at Base Camp for weeks. He was two vertical miles below Everest's summit, where fear, chaos, and death had taken hold.

Filming on Mount Everest was my dream. The scale and drama of climbing the world's tallest mountain is picture-perfect for the giant IMAX screen, but it comes at a cost. The cold and the elevation challenge everyone, but especially large format camera teams using our heavy, expensive, and imperfect equipment. We planned for every contingency, not only for safety but to ensure success. I stayed in California to receive the IMAX footage, review and rank each shot, and communicate with the team on the mountain what we still needed. We had the best-funded team: the best Sherpas, climbing and camera team, radios and satellite phones, medical and Base Camp support. Yet the events on May 10 went beyond our imagination.

From Base Camp, Brad reported that our film team was safe at Camp II. David Breashears, Robert Schauer, and Ed Viesturs were making all the right decisions. As the Everest tragedy unfolded, I was very proud of our team. They put their cameras down, shared our oxygen stashed in tents at Camp IV, used our radios and satellite phones to communicate up and down the mountain, and helped rescue the injured.

From far away, my heart was with them. They had only begun to grieve their lost friends. Back at Base Camp days later, they were faced with the choice of whether to climb the mountain—and make the movie—or go home. On the satellite phone with David and Brad, there was no pressure from me. I reassured them we could come back next year; we'd budgeted for failure in 1996.

Greg MacGillivray (right, with Robert Schauer) spent two years editing the film and testing it with audiences.

That David, Robert, Ed, Jamling, Araceli, and our Sherpas picked up the IMAX camera and endeavored back to the highest place on Earth—well, the whole experience became more than just a movie. It was a real-life story of heartbreak, courage, and personal triumph.

We worked two years in post-production and editing to get the story right. Writers Stephen Judson and Tim Cahill crafted perhaps 20 versions of the film, which we tested and re-tested with audiences. Our promotional push by far outdistanced any other IMAX film ever released.

Everest became the most successful documentary in history, not only because our heroic team picked up the camera again and reached the summit or because we spent the time and money editing the film until I was 100 percent satisfied. *Everest* became a blockbuster for many reasons, but mostly because our audience knows and recognizes those uniquely human qualities—fear, love, strength, courage, and loss—that played out so powerfully on the giant screen. These are the mountaintop experiences in our own lives, and we can all recognize and feel the positives and negatives, the clarity and turmoil of those moments.

A porter carries heavy loads through Everest Base Camp.

how you perform and how you handle a situation that may be life threatening. There's a reward for your effort and a lot of fatigue, too, but I even like the fatigue. I like to wake up in the morning feeling stronger than I was the day before."

Clearly, some climbers are on a quest and set out not so much to conquer a physical obstacle as to attain a new level of understanding of themselves. Climbing a high mountain may be modern man's outlet for the classic hero's struggle codified by Joseph Campbell: approaching, confronting, and then overcoming the weaknesses and demons that haunt us and obstruct us. For this quest, Everest offers the ideal tableau.

The Sherpas and other Himalayan Buddhists express this struggle in the form of pilgrimage and in daily rituals. They seek spiritual liberation, but they will settle for gaining merit. The Sherpa people understand what the foreign climbers are seeking. They're just not sure that climbing mountains is the best way to find it.

Some climbers who attempt Everest appear to be searching for a sense of power and achievement, for fame and attention. The Sherpas question whether these are proper motivations for being on the mountain. Luck, skill, desire, and money are not sufficient to get one to the top. In order to succeed consistently, the Sherpas say, one's motivation must be pure. They believe Everest and Khumbu's mountains are the domains of gods and goddesses. The mountains exist as much in the realm of the spiritual as they do the physical. Both groups—Sherpas and foreign climbers—share the recognition that humans did not create the Himalaya and that they are beyond man's control.

A CROWD GATHERS

In the Kathmandu market, the team ran across New Zealand guide Rob Hall, who claimed to have

know what to do with it," one Sherpa offered. Paradoxically, though religion forms the fabric of the Sherpas' lives, it may be the foreigners who bring a more introspective, philosophical approach to the mountain.

"Willi Unsoeld, my articulate climbing companion on the West Ridge in 1963, saw in Everest the values of dreaming, striving, risk, going beyond oneself, and caring for our earth and our relationship to it," wrote Tom Hornbein.

Breashears agrees. "Climbing Everest is about the deprivations, the challenge, the sheer physical beauty, the movement and rhythm. And it's partly about risk. You learn about yourself, about what happens when you abandon comfort and warmth and a daily routine, the tyranny of the urgent. You learn

escorted 39 climbers to the summit of Everest—more than the total number of people that summited during the 20-year period following the first climb, in 1953. This year, he brought eight clients, two more than he had ever brought to the mountain. One of them was Jon Krakauer, sent there to write about the experience, and the world of guided climbing, for *Outside* magazine.

American guide Scott Fischer also arrived with a team of guides and clients. Fischer had been on Everest once before, in 1994, when he summited without oxygen. This year his Seattle-based company, Mountain Madness, had taken on several clients, among them New York adventurer and NBC correspondent Sandy Hill Pittman, who, if she summited Everest, would have successfully climbed all "Seven Summits," the highest mountain on each continent. Another client was climbing legend Pete Schoening, widely known as a hero for having saved the lives of six team members high on K2, in 1953. If Schoening were to reach the summit, he would be the oldest person to climb Everest, at 68.

At the expedition staging area in the crowded center of Kathmandu, the climbers and Sherpas moved bundles of equipment, gas cylinders, duffels, and boxes of food, while Ed and Paula logged each item. Shooing away curious jungle crows that squawked and hopped about, they stood back and scrutinized the gear and the confusion.

> 66
> Nobody can go there without thinking that this is way cool just to be able to climb on this thing. Just that idea that **you're actually going to put your feet on Everest** . . . I don't care whether you're a climber or not a climber. That's big stuff.
>
> ~BECK WEATHERS,
> *IN STORM OVER EVEREST,* 2008 FILM
> 99

"We organized our wedding at the same time we prepared for the expedition," Paula said. "It *was* hectic."

Calculating quantities, locating supplies, and buying and packing the food and equipment became a full-time job for three months. Three tons of gear were shipped from Seattle: 57 food boxes, 30 climbing hardware and tent loads (including over 40 tents and 50 sleeping pads), 5 science cases, 3,000 feet of rope, 75 bottles of oxygen, hundreds of rolls of toilet paper, and 47 tins of Spam. The film gear was shipped separately. Propane, kerosene, gasoline, and additional food and supplies would be purchased in Kathmandu. Eventually, 250 loads would have to be transported to Base Camp by helicopter, yak, and porter.

MacGillivray Freeman's Everest Film Expedition, not including the science and film components, would cost nearly three-quarters of a million dollars—a significant location expense. David Breashears was determined to make the summit, but early on both he and Greg MacGillivray resolved that he wouldn't allow the high stakes of the expedition to compromise their commitment to safety and caution.

A POPULAR PEAK

The team was fortunate to have picked a year when permits to climb Everest from the Nepal side were

---

FLASH FORWARD **DAVID BREASHEARS**

Breashears returned to Everest in 1997 to shoot a documentary for PBS, and again in 2004 for his documentary *Storm Over Everest,* in which survivors of the 1996 disaster reflect on their experiences. He has written several books and more recently, founded GlacierWorks, a nonprofit organization that uses cutting-edge technology to create unprecedented megapixel images of the Himalaya and exhibits them internationally to raise awareness about climate change in the region. He has spent several years advising and co-producing Universal Pictures' 2015 *Everest* movie, which retells the story of 1996.

Kathmandu's market at Asan Tol is always bustling, which tends to make any filming there an interesting challenge.

available on relatively short notice. Prior to 1978, only one expedition per route was allowed each season, and the waiting list for the South Col route, considered to be the easiest, was more than five years long. But in that year, the Mountaineering Section of Nepal's Ministry of Tourism opened up south-side routes to more than one climbing team—possibly after they observed that multiple teams were climbing from the north side of the mountain, in Tibet.

With only a nominal fee per expedition and few limitations, the number of groups and climbers increased through the 1980s—until the spring season of 1993 when 15 teams, comprising nearly 300 climbers, attempted Everest from the south. The following season, the Ministry of Tourism limited the number of teams to four, while increasing the royalty to $50,000 per expedition of up to five members, plus $10,000 for each additional member, to a maximum of seven.

In the spring of 1996, rather than impose a ceiling on the number of teams, the government increased the fee to $70,000 per seven-member expedition, plus $10,000 for each additional member, to a maximum of 12. As anticipated, the new policy boosted mountaineering revenues. During the spring of 1996, Everest climbing royalties generated more than $800,000, a large sum for a developing country. Many have complained that only a fraction of this amount has been allocated to environmental conservation or mountain safety, and little has trickled down to the local people.

For a client, the average going rate now ranges from $30,000 to $70,000, and organizing a large expedition can cost over a half million dollars. When Charles Houston, physiology adviser to the film, climbed K2 in 1938, the round-trip cost for the entire expedition was $9,500. The second attempt he led, in 1953, cost $35,000.

Attracted by the film's potential to promote tourism, the government of Nepal issued the IMAX *Everest* team a permit in the early spring of 1996. At the time, Breashears had no idea that his group would be joined on the mountain by 13 other teams, all climbing on the same route and during the same narrow window in May when good weather was expected. The two largest groups alone, those led by Scott Fischer and Rob Hall, would be placing 22 guides and clients and nearly as many Sherpas on a single route up the mountain.

ASAN TOL AND THE CITY

The team slalomed their way through a maze of people to the very heart of Kathmandu: the busy market area of Asan Tol. Regardless of their destination in the city, everyone intersects at this six-way hub of narrow alleyways, a crossroad of culture and color.

Asan Tol's Annapurna ("Goddess of Abundance of Grain") Temple is appropriately surrounded by burlap sacks of grain, the tops neatly rolled back by merchants for buyers to inspect. Ministers, mendicants, visiting hill people, and pilgrims ring the temple's bells and make offerings to the Hindu and Buddhist deities, then jostle their way through rickshaws, overloaded pushcarts, and breeding bulls that range freely, grazing on vegetable scraps and cardboard. The smells of incense and rotting vegetables meld in a thick, organic vapor.

The self-proclaimed Global Emperor, a Kathmandu temple pundit and eccentric, greeted David

Jamling and Sumiyo made sure to spin prayer wheels like these in search of blessings and good fortune.

The colorful thrum never seems to ebb at hubs like Kathmandu's Trailokya Mohan Narayan Temple.

Breashears in an alley near the temple and handed him playing-card-size pictures of deities of the Hindu pantheon, with his "global messages" inscribed on the back. David listened carefully as he imparted advice that contained, without irony, the two most repeated axioms of life in Nepal: "Oh, no, sir, you can't do that here" and "Here, my good man, *anything* is possible."

Filming in Kathmandu proved both axioms. Steve Judson rapidly adjusted to the chaotic, medieval location with his sense of humor intact. "The first few times I called for 'action,' everybody stopped and looked at me. Finally, someone informed me that the Nepali term *ek chin* means 'wait a minute'!"

The teetering, overbuilt character of the old section of Kathmandu lent a mild foreboding to the proceedings. The valley is situated above a huge earthquake fault that underlies most of the Himalaya, and some

of the valley's residents are old enough to remember when the city was devastated by the Great Bihar Earthquake of 1934, a year they still count time from. In 1996, some seismologists believed that the next "great" earthquake would devestate the crowded city; in 2015, a M 7.9 earthquake did just that.

One concerned citizen is Kathmandu building engineer Hemant Aryal. He recognizes that the cantilever design of many buildings has created welcome space in the city's cramped core. But because the overhangs of the cantilevers can be no wider than three feet, the owners tend to construct the walls with bricks stacked on their sides. In addition, the quality of cement mortar is "variable."

"The bricks can be easily dislodged by even the smallest horizontal thrust," Mr. Aryal writes. "In a quake, as people run out of their houses to escape, they will be greeted by a rain of bricks."

BORN TO CLIMB

Born in 1965, Jamling, short for Jambuling Yandak, or "world-famed," was the climbing leader for the Everest Film Expedition. His father, Tenzing Norgay, made the first ascent of Mount Everest with Edmund Hillary, in 1953.

My father, Tenzing Norgay, was my mentor and role model. When I was young, he took me trekking in the Sikkim Himalaya, where he taught me to climb. At age six I scrambled up a peak with him.

Traditionally, Sherpa sons follow in their fathers' footsteps. But when I told my father of my dream to climb Everest, he said, "Why? I climbed so my children wouldn't have to—so you can get a good education and not have to carry loads in the mountains, risking your life." That's what he wanted: to give us everything.

Once I started climbing, though, he didn't discourage me. At St. Paul's School in Darjiling I organized rock-climbing demonstrations. Climbing was in my blood, it seems.

In 1984, the Indian Everest Expedition put the first Indian woman, Bachendri Pal, on the summit. I was 18 and had wanted to join that expedition. I had hoped to be the youngest person to climb Everest. I was a pilgrim craving reunion with the mountain that drew me, just as I am now. But my father was sick, and I decided not to go.

I then came to the United States to study at Northland College in Wisconsin, where my father had received an honorary law degree in 1973.

America was exciting and stimulating, but something was missing. My father died in 1986, and in 1992, while my two brothers, one sister, and I were living in the U.S., my mother died. Our roots in the Himalaya were about to wither, so I chose to return.

With the death of my parents, my determination to climb Everest became even stronger. I organized a small expedition in 1993 to commemorate the 40th anniversary of my father's Everest climb. In my heart I knew that reaching the summit was only a matter of time.

I became engaged to my fiancée Soyang, whom I had gone to school with in Darjiling. Our parents were good friends, and they arranged the marriage—sort of. Even in school, I always knew I'd marry her one day. But she didn't always know of my dream of climbing Everest.

Jamling's father, Tenzing Norgay, stands triumphant at the summit of Mount Everest.

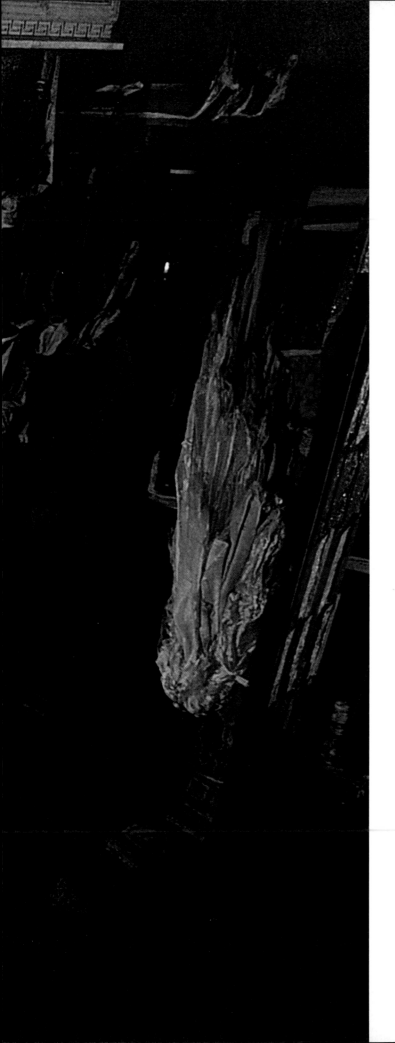

Additionally, Kathmandu's narrow streets are festooned with a labyrinth of frayed electrical wires that will increase the existing fire hazard from cooking fires. And after a quake, fire trucks won't be able to negotiate the narrow, brick-clogged streets.

Perhaps prayer will help. Though Kathmandu is virtually choked with motor vehicles and factories, the valley is still dotted with ancient power spots—geomantic focal points of spiritual energy that valley residents believe confer blessings on those who frequent them.

The team members took a break from their stockpiling of supplies to visit Swayambhunath, the monkey temple. For Jamling, Sumiyo, and the Sherpas—all Buddhists—this was a chance to prepare in another way: by making offerings to the deities of this holy site. The stupa of Swayambhunath, an ancient hilltop shrine, is sacred to both the Hindus, who entered Nepal from the south centuries ago, and the Buddhists, who came from the north. Swayambhunath means "self-arisen," and legend says that the hill on which the stupa is located spontaneously emerged from the lake bed that is now the Kathmandu valley. Joining the daily stream of supplicants, Jamling and Sumiyo ascended the 365 stairs to the stupa. They prayed and threw grain from bamboo trays to the hundreds of pigeons and rhesus monkeys that long ago claimed Swayambhunath as their home. These offerings of life bring *sonam*, or spiritual merit, which contributes to a more favorable rebirth.

As they circumambulated the stupa dome, they spun prayer wheels for blessings and good fortune. It is said that the copper repoussé wheels, packed with prayers and mantras block-printed on hundreds of scrolled rice paper folios, release the written invocations heavenward with each revolution. A handful of foreign Buddhists, mixing easily with the locals, also chanted and spun.

The team frantically tried to fit all the color and action into the widest-angle lens, while monkeys eyed

1996: The glowing lights of 25,000 butter lamps at the Great Stupa of Bodhnath.

25,000 BUTTER LAMPS

Jamling was saving some of his offerings for the stupa of Bodhnath, the nerve center and soul of a mostly Tibetan community on the east side of Kathmandu. The stupa's stone skirt has been worn by countless circuits of murmuring, faithful Buddhists, the soles of their buffalo-hide boots scuffing through a thin layer of dust. Motorized traffic, now blocked from entry, growls and shrieks impatiently outside the gates.

For the success of the expedition, but mainly for its protection and safety, Jamling sponsored the lighting of 25,000 butter lamps at the stupa. For most of the day on March 17, Audrey Salkeld and Paula Viesturs worked with 30 of the team Sherpas, twisting cotton wicks and rustling up shallow pottery cups that would function as lamps. By late afternoon, they had arranged them along the outline of the three main tiers of the mandala-shaped stupa.

The Sherpas—and hundreds of devout bystanders, mostly Tibetan—gathered to light the rows of golden lamps. They filled the clay receptacles with their own melted butter, poured from Chinese vacuum flasks. To forfeit consumption of a valuable commodity such as butter, Jamling noted, demonstrates that one is willing to nourish the gods before oneself.

The angled surface of the terraces became slick with spilled butter, and the lamps ignited with difficulty. When the last one was lit, the climbers, film-makers, Sherpas, and support staff climbed a narrow

the film gear. David reminded Brad Ohlund and Robert Schauer not to leave lenses or equipment unattended, lest they be lifted by these acquisitive rogues.

Jamling paused to purchase a long roll of colorful prayer flags that he planned to unfurl on the summit after having them blessed by a high lama.

For Jamling, the nun's words were comforting. His wife, Soyang, was not entirely pleased with his Everest plans, and she remained quietly worried. "I asked Soyang to give me one chance to climb it, so that we wouldn't have regrets later," he said. "She agreed, but on one condition: that I consult her family's guru, a Tibetan lama, and request a *mo*, a divination. Geshé Rimpoche is an incarnate lama and is known for his accurate *mos*. Even the staff of embassies in Kathmandu go to him for advice." Jamling paused. "I was afraid he'd tell me not to go."

At Geshé Rimpoche's monastery, Jamling climbed several flights of creaking wooden stairs and entered a humble room, barely large enough to hold a table, bed, and two or three visitors. Rimpoche, swathed in maroon and brocade robes, was sitting cross-legged on the bed. He motioned Jamling to sit and called his assistant to bring tea. He then consulted his rosary.

stairway to the roof of an adjacent building. Finally, the entire team had come together in one place. They hugged and filmed as the golden light infused in them a sense of calm, good fortune, warmth, and equanimity, if not a feeling of proximity to the gods. Beyond the stupa, the lights of landing airplanes winked at Venus, which sat placidly above the sunset.

Even a small breeze can make it impossible to light the lamps or keep them lit. For two nights before the ceremony, Steve and David had scouted the stupa and were twice reminded by the caretakers that it was too windy to consider a butter lamp ceremony. Before the team gathered on the rooftop, a Buddhist nun had approached Jamling with a broad smile and bowed her head slightly in gratitude. She said that although the afternoon had been quite windy, it was propitious that the wind stopped. The gods were looking favorably on Jamling's and the expedition's offering.

Young Buddhist monks watch Mahakala Puja, a ritual for clearing old obstacles away, at Kathmandu's Kopan monastery.

The journey to Everest may bring one past sadhus, who choose a life of renunciation of the material world.

When he looked up from the string of 108 beads, he said, "Go ahead: You'll be successful, it looks favorable." He smiled, aware of Jamling's strong desire to climb the mountain.

Jamling asked Rimpoche for a *puja*, a propitiatory ritual, as well. At Soyang's family house in Kathmandu, Rimpoche performed a long-life ceremony and studied the Tibetan almanac to prescribe the most opportune day for him to depart the house. Jamling followed his words precisely, unwilling to chance anything.

The morning of the team's departure, Geshé Rimpoche gave Jamling some powder and blessed grains of sand to sprinkle in dangerous places—wherever he might feel afraid, such as avalanche-prone areas and the Khumbu Icefall. He also gave Jamling a tiny cloth bag containing hair and other relics of

> ❝
> To Miyolang-sangma, lady of the vast, unchanging white snows
> . . . **accomplish all the work** we have entrusted you!
>
> ~A PRAYER FOR THE
> LOCAL GODS
> ❞

high lamas, to place on the summit. Most importantly, Rimpoche presented him with a protective *sung-wa* amulet, a piece of handmade paper inscribed with astrological designs and religious symbols, then folded precisely and bound by a crosshatch of colored threads. Jamling wrapped the amulet in plastic, to protect it from sweat and dirt, and had it sewn into a yellow brocade bag, along with some "long life" pills.

Jamling was greatly relieved. Before leaving Darjiling, he had consulted Chatrul Rimpoche—his own family's guru—who had also done a mo. Jamling hadn't mentioned that mo's disconcerting results to Soyang.

Sunlight bathes the jagged peaks of Kangtega and Thamserku, looming giants of the Khumbu region.

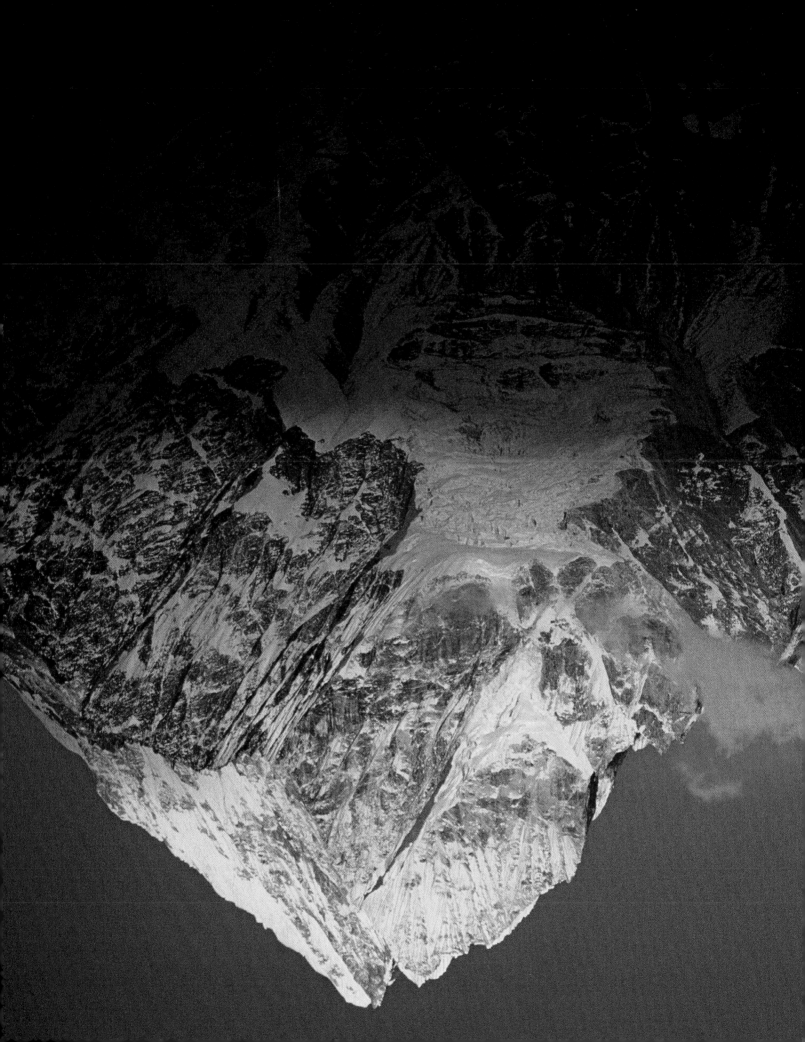

"Chatrul Rimpoche didn't tell me not to go, but he said Everest looked a little uncertain this year. I could tell that he saw something difficult in the prayer beads—danger, it seemed. He said nothing more, other than to be careful and that he'd pray for us."

Even Jamling was aware that divinations, though often accurate, could be interpreted in several ways. More important, he must maintain pure intentions on the mountain, the clarity of purpose and dedication that Buddhists refer to as "right motivation."

TO KHUMBU

The team was prepared, officially, logistically, physically, and spiritually. Only last-minute details remained: constructing a frame for Roger's solar panels, signing postcards, and changing dollars into bags of rupees for paying porters and yak drivers. At least they wouldn't have to carry baskets of heavy coins, as Charles Houston did with the first party of foreigners to enter Khumbu, in 1950. The Sherpas had by then overcome their distrust of paper money and will now even accept traveler's checks.

On March 20, the team assembled at the Kathmandu airport and climbed into a hulking Russian Mi-17 helicopter, a relic from the Afghan War, and squeezed onto fold-down benches along the windows. As the Mi-17 noisily lifted off, the team's whoops and chants nearly drowned out the rotor blades. Jangbu, a climbing Sherpa and Wongchu's right-hand man, shook his head skeptically. "Too much vibration."

The team was informed that the helicopters had been used as air taxis for years in the former Soviet Union. As the whirling blades strobed the faces of the group, Araceli looked around nervously. "For how many years?" her worried face seemed to ask. She noticed the paratroopers' clip line leading to the door. The panel behind it was worn shiny from apparent decades of use.

The chopper crossed the end of the runway and its shadow leaped out over the rice paddies. It rolled

left, to the east, headed for the airstrip of Lukla in the region of Solu-Khumbu, the northern part of which is termed "Khumbu."

As the helicopter rose above the diffuse fog blanketing the valley, the Himalaya mountains emerged. Their crystalline forms pushed against a navy blue sky as if visibly being thrust upward by the colliding landmasses of India and Eurasia. Like the

1996: After a 40-minute copter flight rather than a two-week trek from Kathmandu to Lukla, the *Everest* film crew began walking to Base Camp and on to the summit, a journey that took three months. (See map p. 65 for wider view.)

42

Himalayan balance of orogeny and erosion, the helicopter's powerful lifting forces were just barely overcoming the relentless pull of gravity.

Because the cabin was unpressurized, the pilots wouldn't fly high enough to avoid the chaotic winds that are channeled skyward by the rumpled foothills. The helicopter leveled out at 11,000 feet, barely higher than its destination, and passed Gauri Sankar.

Though this 23,442-foot sacred mountain has been climbed, the Hindus say that Shiva, the God of Destruction, occupies the top of its craggy throne. His consort Gauri sits on the nearby south summit.

Everest is one of the mountains most revered by Sherpa Buddhists. They call it Chomolungma—commonly translated as "Mother Goddess of the World" or "Maiden of the Wind," and known to the Nepalis

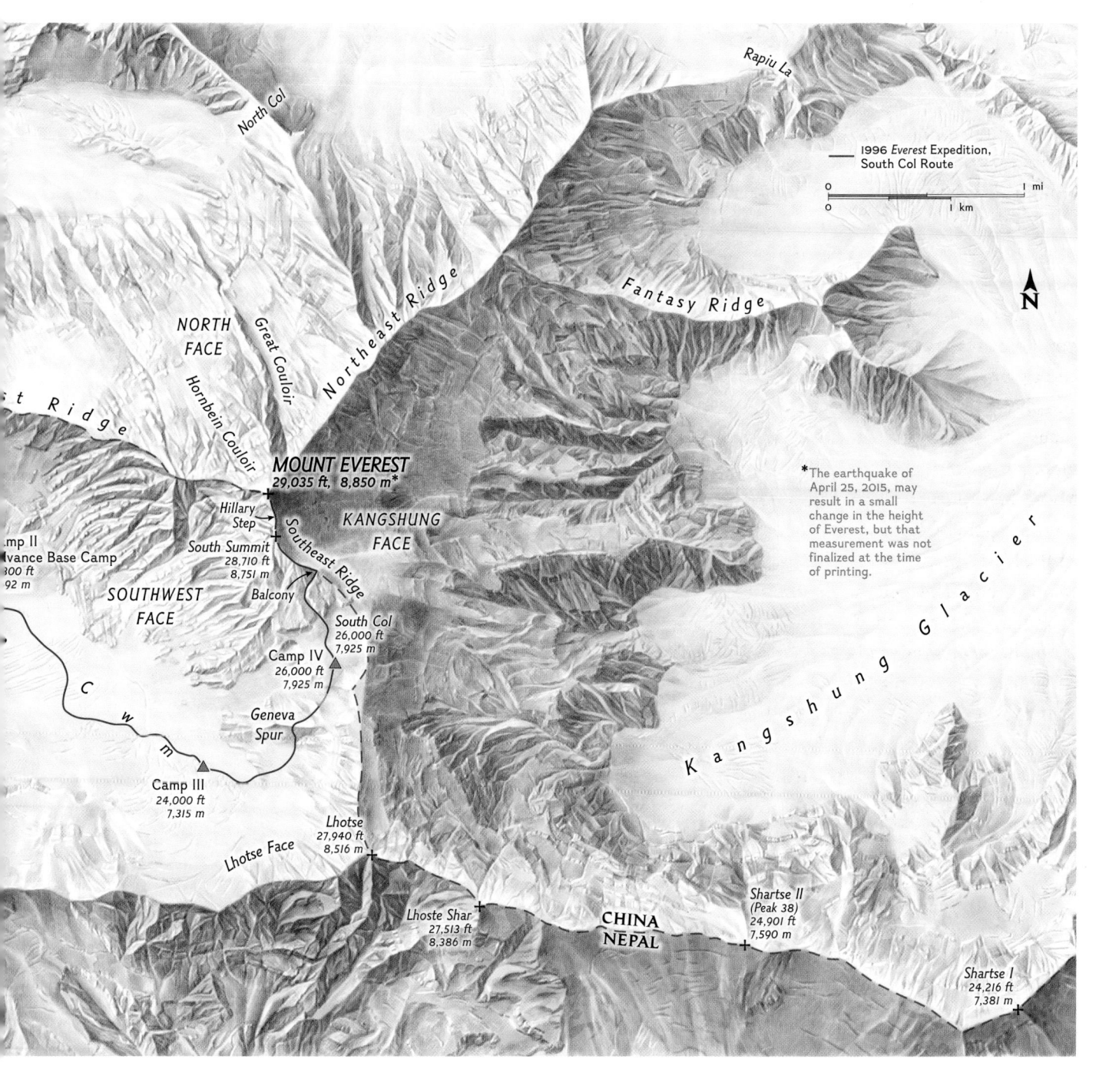

1996 *Everest* Expedition, South Col Route

Rapiu La

North Col

Fantasy Ridge

N

NORTH FACE

Great Couloir

Northeast Ridge

Hornbein Couloir

t Ridge

MOUNT EVEREST
29,035 ft, 8,850 m*

Hillary Step

KANGSHUNG FACE

South Summit
28,710 ft
8,751 m

Southeast Ridge

mp II
vance Base Camp
300 ft
92 m

Balcony

SOUTHWEST FACE

South Col
26,000 ft
7,925 m

Camp IV
26,000 ft
7,925 m

*The earthquake of April 25, 2015, may result in a small change in the height of Everest, but that measurement was not finalized at the time of printing.

Kangshung Glacier

C
w
m

Geneva Spur

Camp III
24,000 ft
7,315 m

Lhotse
27,940 ft
8,516 m

Lhotse Face

Lhoste Shar
27,513 ft
8,386 m

CHINA
NEPAL

Shartse II
(Peak 38)
24,901 ft
7,590 m

Shartse I
24,216 ft
7,381 m

Lukla airstrip's eight degrees of pitch intimidates pilots, especially since it dead-ends in a rock wall.

as Sagarmatha. From the team's distance, the mountain looked miniature as it emerged on the northeast horizon, but a distinctive white plume blew from the summit like a *kata* blessing scarf. Jangbu said he wondered why anyone would want to rename a mountain as sacred and majestic as Chomolungma after a human.

In the valley of the Dudh Kosi (Milk River—named for its glacial silt), the chopper turned north and followed the Everest trek route to Lukla. From above, the airstrip looked much steeper than the eight degrees of pitch that has intimidated many pilots, and it dead-ends in a sheer wall of rock. If fixed-wing pilots overshoot it, they'll have a first-hand encounter with the Himalaya itself.

The first airplane landing at Lukla was made by Emil Wick in 1964. David and other veteran climbers still tell stories of this legendary Swiss pilot, who was stationed in Nepal by the Pilatus Porter factory to fly and maintain its high-performance plane. Wick once flew to 32,000 feet, directly over Everest and far above the plane's rated ceiling, while one passenger opened the door for filming. That height could be reached, Wick said, only by seeking out and catching the updrafts that funnel up Everest's Western Cwm to the South Col. After dropping 20,000 feet in a near free fall, Wick sneaked up on the Tengboche monastery—lower than the level of the cupola—and turned to tell his partly thrilled, partly horrified riders, "I want to see if I can spin a few prayer wheels this time." He then jerked the wings to a vertical angle to avoid clipping the tops of two tall prayer-flag poles, while people on the ground ran for cover.

By 1996, the plane's engine had been converted from piston to turbine—a mixed blessing, Emil said, because turbine-powered planes shouldn't be flown upside down.

The team climbed out of the monstrous Russian chopper on unsteady legs. At 9,000 feet, the Lukla air was cool and decidedly thinner. Aromas of juniper fires, yak dung, and turboprop exhaust washed over them, displaced briefly by a light breeze of nostril-tingling glacial air flowing down from Khumbu and Tibet. The smell of Everest.

Moments later, a siren alerted the gawkers and livestock on the runway, and the Mi-17 lifted off in a glorious cloud of dust—to the Sherpas, a wonderful sign of progress.

In the fall of 1964, anthropologist Jim Fisher and an associate completed survey work and land negotiations before grading a sloping meadow to create the Lukla airstrip. It was intended as an access point for building materials and medical supplies for the hospital in Khunde, built in 1966 by Sir Edmund Hillary's Himalayan Trust.

A two-week walk had suddenly been reduced to a forty-minute flight. Now, half a kilometer of lodges and shops line the main route that leads out of town. Understandably, the Lukla people are rallying to halt the growing Russian helicopter traffic to the Syangboche airstrip, to the north. Because Syangboche is located closer to Everest, trekkers can now bypass Lukla altogether.

ON THE TRAIL

Ed, Jamling, and Jangbu oversaw the loading of *zopkios*, male yak-cow crossbreeds that are better adapted than yaks to carrying loads at elevations below 12,000 feet. Slowly, the team moved out of town and headed up the Dudh Kosi

> **66**
> The mountain is so high and so indifferent it calls upon every climber, at one time or another, to rise to **his or her better self.**
>
> ~MARK JENKINS,
> "MAXED OUT
> ON EVEREST"
> **99**

valley. Emerald fields of new wheat and bright yellow blooming mustard formed a quilt along the deep ravine. Lowland porters hunkered beneath oversize loads, their feet the color and texture of elephant hide, with calluses the thickness of sneaker soles. From homes and tea shops perched on terraces along the trail, grandmothers carrying infants in cradles waved the Sherpas in for tea.

Along the Dudh Kosi, white-capped redstarts darted and skimmed about the river rocks, while an ouzel (brown dipper) stood on a rock doing its mysterious deep knee bends, perhaps to gain a better perspective on prey beneath the water. Grandalas in their blue-black formal wear hopped about on the pine forest duff above the river. In clearings of potato fields, strikingly black-and-white-striped hoopoes foraged.

The temperate climate put Audrey in mind of a British country garden, and she lingered among the drumstick primulas and tiny gentians carpeting the margins of the path. Yellow cinquefoil poked out of crevices in the trail, and tiny baby-blue butterflies danced in spirals.

(Continued on page 48)

Gouged by nature and terraced by man, the ridges of the southern Himalaya comprise a land of erosion and earthquakes.

Namche Bazar's open-air market boasts piles of meat and vegetables, as well as porters looking to tempt passersby with their produce.

mountain peaks, you are mostly viewing the absence of material between them."

The rivers carry away the mountains in the form of solutions (chemically dissolved rocks), suspended rocks (mud and sand), and bed load (boulders rolled along the bottom). "We can measure the amount of eroded rock from the rate that reservoirs fill with sediment," Roger explained. "But this is only an approximate gauge, because we believe most erosion occurs during very heavy rainfalls that may happen only once per century—perhaps when we aren't measuring.

"For most of Nepal's river basins, the overall erosion rate is about two millimeters per year. Although we have measured uplift rates of three millimeters per year in the foothills and rates of five to eight millimeters per year in the high mountains, these rates are very localized."

But three centuries of erosion can virtually be reversed during the few moments of rapid uplift that occurs during a great Himalayan earthquake, when plates shift and faults realign.

As the trail went from forest to village, several species of rhododendron appeared, along with blooming, crispy-white bridal magnolias and blushing pink Himalayan cherry.

The team continued north to Phakding, a small community straddling two sides of the Dudh Kosi, connected by a rickety bridge. The gray riverbanks revealed that the glacial till of the valley bottom had been recently scoured by a large flood.

SILT

Geologist Roger Bilham kept his eye to the ground and to the cliff sides, seeming to look below their surfaces. The rocks offered evidence of the great continental collision that is still occurring.

About 50 million years ago, the Indian continental plate collided with Eurasia, and was forced into it and beneath it. The compression and uplift from this collision—plus accretions of material scraped off the Indian plate—resulted in the reason Roger and the expedition are here: the Himalaya.

"The most remarkable process occurring here is not so much the growth of the mountains," Roger said, "but their rapid *erosion*. When you observe a series of

> " One day's exposure to the mountains is **better than a cartload of books.**
>
> ~JOHN MUIR,
>
> WILDERNESS ADVOCATE "

ONWARD

The team was leaving the area called Pharak and entering Khumbu, the region that since 1976 has also defined the boundaries of Sagarmatha National Park. Schematically, Khumbu is funnel shaped, and the only access, other than across treacherous glaciated passes above 18,000 feet, is past the park entrance station at Monjo. This hamlet is at the park's lowest point, at 9,200 feet on the Dudh Kosi.

It's all uphill from here. With steady, rocking gaits,

(previous spread) The glowing lights of Namche Bazar, a village perched at 11,300 feet and shadowed by Kwangde peak
(right) People and zopkios, hybrid yak bulls, wind through rhododendron forests near Tengboche.

48

climbers and yaks made their way up 2,000 vertical feet toward Namche Bazar. At places along the steep switchbacks the narrow trail drops away 1,000 feet or more. "That's where I learned the first lesson of trekking," Steve Judson said. "Never stand between a yak and a sheer drop-off."

Namche, at 11,300 feet, sits on a terrace far above the river that formed it and is overshadowed by the nearby peak of Kwangde, at 20,298 feet. With Jeff Lowe in 1982, Breashears climbed Kwangde's north face, a difficult new route, alpine style—one of the hardest technical climbs ever made in the Himalaya.

Namche is Khumbu's largest village, a market town of a hundred houses and a score of lodges—some of them four stories tall, with 360-degree-view restaurants. There's a bank, offices, shops, and a dental clinic, established with aid from the American Himalayan Foundation, where two young Western-trained Sherpas stay busy doing fillings and other dental work for Khumbu villagers and government staff.

Namche's bustling Saturday market exemplifies free enterprise. Sides of buffalo meat, sacks of grain, and bamboo baskets filled with vegetables and tangerines line the terraces at the edge of town, a porter manning each basket.

A luxurious trek can be outfitted from leftover expedition supplies for sale in Namche shops. After a Spanish expedition, the town was awash in tins of marinated trout from Catalonia. One Sherpa cook nearly gave away a drum full of large glass bottles of Black Sea caviar he had inherited from the retreating Soviet team. "Fish eggs," the cook scoffed.

On the steep trail that leads out of Namche to Khumjung, the team was buzzed by a squadron of snow pigeons, hugging the valleys and ridges, their sudden *whoosh* catching the climbers by surprise around a blind corner. The white pigeons banked into a turn and momentarily disappeared, then reappeared heading in the opposite direction, this time preceded by their shadows.

The peak of Ama Dablam hovers above a swath of prayer flags at a stupa in Khumbu.

CHAPTER TWO

TO BASE CAMP BY YAK TRAIN

The mountains enclosing Khumbu are so disorientingly high, and the trails so uneven, that it's easy to lose your balance on the flagstones that line the trail, rocks worn into smooth round shapes by centuries of foot travel. Taking in Khumbu for the first time, Roger Bilham marveled at the forces that created what he referred to as "this giant museum of metamorphic petrology." He pulled out his notebook and cataloged Khumbu's geological riches: "harder

crystals protrude from their matrix of quartz and plagioclase . . . needles of black epidote, luminous spheres of red garnet and hexagonal bars of blue beryl . . ."

Above the Syangboche airstrip, the team paused at a large domed stupa—the sort of monument that Sherpas and Tibetans term a *chorten* ("receptacle of offerings"). David Breashears looked up at the painted eyes of the Buddha Ratnasambhava and

followed their gaze to the south, where tiers of bluish ridges faded into hazy white sky above the Gangetic Plain of India.

"With all the smoke from the industry and cooking fires of India, the surveyors of the Great Trig Survey would have a hell of a time getting a clear line of sight to the Himalaya today," David observed. The haze *(Continued on page 56)*

Climbers pay their respects at the Tenzing Norgay memorial chorten en route to Base Camp.

was confined to the south, but during his test filming in Khumbu a year earlier, an unusual pall had threatened to dull even Mount Everest's splendor.

The team continued north 20 minutes to Khumjung, a village of a hundred houses cradled in the shadow of Khumbila, a scraggy 18,900-foot peak that embodies Khumbu's sacred protector god. They entered the town through the *kani*, a covered stone entryway. The meditating and levitating deities pictured on its ceiling panels are meant to deter evil spirits that might attempt to follow those who enter—while symbolically introducing visitors to the sacred nature of their surroundings.

HOSPITALITY IN KHUMJUNG

The team arrived at the home of David's old friends Nima Tenzing and his wife Pema Chamji, where they would stay for several nights. Nima was a kitchen boy for a trekking company when David

> **❝**
> And in subjecting ourselves to week after week of toil, tedium and suffering, it struck me that **most of us were probably seeking** above all else, something like **a state of grace.**
> ~JON KRAKAUER,
> *INTO THIN AIR*
> **❞**

first met him in 1979, and he later worked as cook and sirdar with David on Kwangde and Everest.

A section of the stone wall enclosing a fallow potato field had been dismantled to admit the zopkios, which would be unloaded and corralled here. Pema Chamji leaned out from a second-story window, smiling; a breeze blew a genial wave along the cloth valance fitted on the lintel above her. She urged everyone upstairs for "tea," which in late afternoon is a euphemism for *chang*, unclarified rice or barley beer.

Shortly after the team had settled in, a walkie-talkie broke, the first malfunction of electronic equipment. Roger excused himself and promptly burrowed into the alligator clamps, voltmeters, and portable oscilloscope he carried with him. But hospitality can't be refused in a Sherpa home, and Pema Chamji interrupted him with a bowl of the nutritious chang. Sherpa tradition dictates that every cup must be refilled at least twice. Roger obliged.

He happily fixed the radio in time for an afternoon jaunt to examine the nearby GPS survey point measured by his research team in previous years. Returning to the house, he became distracted counting tree growth rings in Nima and Pema Chamji's firewood pile. The oldest were wind-stunted, high-altitude junipers, 120 years old. He had found similar trees in the Karakorum as old as 1,300 years.

"Old trees can tell us about past changes in Himalayan weather," Roger explained. "Wet years produce more growth, and thicker rings. Occasionally, the rings tell us about earthquakes, too: A quake might accelerate hillside creep, which alters the symmetry of that year's growth ring."

(previous spread) 1996: Yaks traditionally heft two 66-pound parcels: The 1996 IMAX *Everest* film team required more than 200 animals.

Prayer flags stretch out through the mists and above the heads of young Buddhist monks outside Khumjung monastery.

Buddhist monks wear saffron-colored *tse-sha*—ceremonial headgear—for the summer festival of Dumje, held in Khumjung.

The heart of Nima and Pema Chamji's house is the firewood hearth, used for cooking meals, distilling alcohol, and warming livestock gruel, and for limited heating. Meat, milk, and food scraps are not burned in the fire for fear of offending the local gods, Khumbu's guardian spirits, especially Me Lha, the deity that resides in the fire. In 1996, chimneys were a recent introduction. More commonly smoke filtered out through the ceilings and windows, depositing a black, shiny resin that greatly extends the longevity of scarce structural timbers and roof shingles.

The large sitting room acted as a communal bedroom for the expedition, and it quickly filled with wet clothes and camera equipment. Nima's own yaks and zopkios were stabled directly below them; Sherpas say the animals' body heat provides some warmth to the floor above.

Liesl Clark, a journalist, had also joined the team. She was covering the expedition for *NOVA Online,* and had already begun compiling news and science dispatches to be sent out by satellite fax. She opened the window and propped the phone near it.

Khumjung had been wired for electricity only a few months earlier, through underground cables, and many residents had begun to cook with electrical hotplates, rice steamers, and microwave ovens, allowing them to conserve precious firewood. For the expedition, the team would use wood, dried yak dung, electricity, kerosene, and propane to cook the countless meals.

THE FAITH OF THE SHERPAS

Each morning, Nima and Pema Chamji engage in a traditional religious routine. Outside on a rock platform they burn a small branch of juniper as a purifying offering. Then, on their altar in the chapel room, they fill seven offering bowls with freshwater—a pledge of their commitment to achieving Buddhahood. Because the devout must relinquish all attachment to their offerings, water is perfect: It has no intrinsic value and can be given freely. Pema Chamji said that it is best if starlight has shone upon the water bowls since they were last filled.

Both perform three prostrations before the altar in a demonstration of respect and abandonment of pride. They then dip the unbroken tip of a juniper bough in an urn of holy water and flick it upward toward the altar three times.

Jamling, too, used their chapel for prayer, and each morning in Khumjung he prostrated and recited mantras, prayerlike invocations that bring merit, mindfulness, and good fortune. Brightly painted in an elaborate mural of deities and demigods, sacred places and hell realms, the walls of the chapel depict a fragment of the map of the Buddhist cosmos. From the chapel's west wall, the goddess Miyolangsangma, who resides on Everest, looked down on Jamling with quiet grace. Riding comfortably on a female tiger, she holds food in her right hand that represents good fortune; in her left she holds a *nyuli*, a mongoose that continually regurgitates precious gems, conferring wealth. This is the goddess whom Jamling's father had worshiped, the goddess who had granted him passage to her sacred summit in 1953.

In contrast to Miyolangsangma's serenity, the panels around her pulsate with menacing, ferocious demons, forever tempting humans away from the path of awareness and devotion. Jamling stood in quiet, unperturbed prayer.

> 66
> Just as a transparent model of the human body consists of a framework of bone and a network of arteries, the **earth's crust is structured** in mountain ridges, rivers, creeks, and gullies.
>
> ~REINHOLD MESSNER,
> *MOUNTAINS FROM SPACE: PEAKS AND RANGES OF THE SEVEN CONTINENTS*
> 99

THE YETI

On the morning of March 24, the team departed for Tengboche. As they switchbacked down to the junction of the Phunki Drangka and Imja Khola Rivers, David spotted a small flock of impeyan pheasants, Nepal's iridescent national bird. Directly overhead, Jamling pointed out a lammergeier, or bearded vulture, riding updrafts near the trail, gliding effortlessly on its nine feet of wingspan. He then told Sumiyo to focus much higher above: A V-configuration of bar-headed geese, migrating over the Himalaya, was passing so far over them that it appeared to barely move.

Araceli wondered aloud if they might see a yeti, a Himalayan abominable snowman. In 1974, Lhakpa Dolma, a Sherpa woman from Khumjung, encountered a yeti while herding yaks in a high Khumbu valley. The moment it saw her, she recounted, it attacked, knocked her out, and left her in a shallow ravine. When she awoke she saw the yeti mutilating her livestock. It killed three of them. Long after, Lhakpa Dolma became edgy and fearful when people around her spoke of the yeti.

Some believe that the yeti are associated with Khumbu Yu Lha, a class of deities known as Dharma Protectors, and that they may be emanations of a wrathful cemetery goddess called Dü-tö Lhamo and other deities. But they are not always dangerous, and are sometimes said to be playful. "Yeti" derives from *ya-té*, "man of the high places," though it is actually surpassed in frightfulness by the *mhi-té*, a long-haired, man-size humanoid that eats people. They say that even a glance from the mhi-té—especially if viewed from below—can cause illness or possibly death.

1996: **Blessing scarves swathe Tengboche's young monks as they pursue a life of awareness and devotion.**

A gateway greets visitors as they leave the forest and come into view of Tengboche monastery.

It is best to avoid saying the names of these dreaded creatures. While chatting with some friends at Base Camp a year earlier, Wongchu recalled, someone uttered "yeti" a fraction of a second before a large avalanche broke off the Lho La, a high pass, and rumbled toward the Khumbu Glacier. The group was momentarily paralyzed, then broke into laughter.

In the 1950s, legendary British climber Eric Shipton photographed footprints he claimed were those of a yeti, and the images were published in the *Times* of London. When queried about Shipton's photos three decades later, Edmund Hillary commented, "I'd have to say—having known Eric very, very well—that in all likelihood he tidied up those tracks."

THE TENGBOCHE MONASTERY

From the bottom of the Imja Khola gorge, the team began the 2,000-vertical-foot ascent of a sandy, forested glacial moraine. Halfway up, Jamling stopped and explained to the climbers the meaning of the carved stone tablets lined neatly beside the trail.

"The Buddhist mantra 'Om Mani Padme Hum,' commonly translated as 'Hail to the Jewel in the Lotus,' is carved on these *mani* stones. It's the mantra of Avalokitesvara—Chenrezig in Tibetan—the Bodhisattva of Compassion. We keep mani stones and stupas—and people, too—to our right as we pass, out of respect."

A few hundred feet farther on, the team emerged from the fir forest and onto a colorful hillside of blooming rhododendrons. They formed a green-and-rose-colored arborway to the Tengboche monastery, atop the moraine at 12,700 feet.

Tengboche was established in 1923 as the first celibate *gompa*, or monastery, in Khumbu. It now houses 45 monks, a record number that some attribute to the Sherpas' new tourism-derived prosperity: With growing incomes, more families can afford to surrender an able-bodied son to the monastery and support him there. Some monks are enrolled as young as seven, though fewer than half will remain in the monastery their entire lives.

This tranquil place was the site of two disasters. The monastery was destroyed in the Great Bihar Earthquake of 1934, and the abbot died shortly after. The monastery was rebuilt, but in 1989 was ravaged by a fire that destroyed almost all the old texts, carvings, murals, and artifacts.

With the aid of Sherpa carpenters, local patrons of the monastery, and grants from the American Himalayan Foundation, the monks have rebuilt the monastery. The Buddhist concepts of patience and nonattachment have been instrumental in Tengboche's survival.

The Sherpas draw much of their religious tradition from Rongbuk monastery in Tibet, located at 16,000 feet on the north side of Everest. Rongbuk was destroyed during the Cultural Revolution, which began 15 years after the Chinese occupation of Tibet in 1951. Fortunately, some of Rongbuk's and Tibetan Buddhism's unique and colorful ceremonies endured in Nepal.

Sumiyo and Araceli stood with Jamling on a terrace below the gompa as he chanted quietly in the direction of its imposing stone walls. "I studied and lived in the United States for ten years," Jamling said, "but wanted to return to the Himalaya to learn more about my own culture. I feel I am completing a circle."

> 66
> Spending time in wild places will always remind you that in the great scheme of nature, **you are just the tiniest smidge** of all the other energies at play.
> ~STEPH DAVIS, IN *MOUNTAIN HEROES: PORTRAITS OF ADVENTURE*
> 99

The deep drone of horns and drums intensified as the three climbed the stairs and traversed the courtyard to the main assembly hall. They halted outside a massive wooden door and removed their shoes. Jamling stepped over the threshold, walked forward three paces, and paused to view the interior of the hall, his hands placed together in supplication. The low vibration was now as palpable as it was audible.

Directly ahead, a formidable statue of Buddha Sakyamuni, the Buddha of the Present, sat 15 feet tall, his gilded shoulders and head extending through an opening in the second floor. Smaller gilded figures stood in attendance in the foreground: disciples Shariputra and Mangalputra, who possess miraculous powers, and the Bodhisattvas Chenrezig and Jambayang. Eight Tatagathas, fully enlightened Buddhas, appeared to levitate within the floor-to-ceiling halo behind the main image. Jamling prostrated three times, lowering himself to the floor and then rising.

Sixteen monks sat in rows facing the main aisle, reciting from long folios opened on low prayer tables. Some rocked slowly as they chanted, while those who had memorized the text continued to pray as they regarded the team with detached interest.

FLASH FORWARD **ARACELI SEGARRA**

Since 1996, Segarra has worked as a motivational speaker, a model, and a children's book author. She has also continued climbing and scrambling over mountains. She has gone on some 30 expeditions, several of which opened up new routes, and worked on several films in the mountains, including *Seven Years in Tibet*. In 2013, she wrote *Not So High, Not So Difficult,* a book to help readers achieve their goals, using climbing as a metaphor for life and including her reflections on the 1996 Everest season.

As his father had done 43 years earlier, Jamling approached the altar and silently presented a long silk kata scarf as an offering of respect to the presiding monk, the Lopon, or Chant Leader. He then handed him the bundle of prayer flags that he hoped to unfurl on the summit.

The Lopon chanted a prayer while touching sacred objects to the bundle. He then poured a handful of blessed barley grains into the bundle's folds: Each kernel is said to contain the qualities and energy of a deity.

For the past three months, the Incarnate Lama had been in strict meditative retreat. When Tenzing Norgay passed through Tengboche on his way to Everest in 1953, the same lama—then 17 years old—was away in Tibet. Tenzing was also blessed by the Lopon of Tengboche.

MANI RIMDU

In the courtyard, the team watched the Tengboche monks demonstrate the Mani Rimdu masked dance ceremony of propitiation and blessing, the dramatic closure to an annual rite that lasts more than two weeks. Along with its ritual functions, Mani Rimdu introduces the lay community to the history and concepts of Buddhism, amid a socially enjoyable gathering.

Early in the ceremony, a yak is bedecked with katas and anointed with butter in a symbolic offering to the Everest goddess, Miyolangsangma. The fortunate yak is then released to wander freely through the hills, never to perform work again.

Before the dances begin, monks in tall, tufted hats and maroon robes lead a formal procession, followed by the masked figure of Mhi Tsering (the Man

Tengboche monks dance in the Mani Rimdu festival, a two-week-long annual Buddhist festival.

THE SHERPA PEOPLE: HERDERS, FARMERS, TRADERS, AND LAMAS

Tibetan texts relate that about 460 years ago, the Sherpas (literally, "people of the east") migrated from the eastern Tibet province of Kham and settled in the shadow of Chomolungma, Mount Everest. They are a comparatively small ethnic group; about 3,000 of the 35,000 Sherpas in Nepal reside in Khumbu.

Traditionally, the Sherpas are seminomadic herders and subsistence farmers. They raise yaks for milk, butter, and hides, and as pack and draft animals, and since the mid-1800s have grown potatoes, thought to have been introduced from British gardens of Darjiling.

During the summer monsoon, Khumbu Sherpas move their yaks and yak crossbreeds to higher elevations. The high *yersa* summer pastures are the last to "green up," and yaks will graze above there, at elevations as high as Everest Base Camp. Sherpas are also traders, and yak trains—somewhat smaller than earlier—still carry grain, butter, buffalo hides, and other items to Tibet across the Nangpa La pass, at 18,753 feet, and return with salt and wool. Trade was curtailed beginning in the 1960s, with the introduction of Indian salt and the Chinese occupation of Tibet, but to some extent tourism has replaced trade as the Sherpas' primary source of income.

Some have suggested that Khumbu's harsh environment sustains and invigorates the Sherpas' ardent faith. Just as the Himalaya themselves were formed by intersections and accretions of geological material, the religion of the Sherpas and other Himalayan peoples is also accretionary—a blending of shamanism, pre-Buddhism, Bön, Buddhism, and local beliefs.

Buddhism has largely prevailed. The Sherpas are of the Nyingmapa, or unreformed, sect of Vajrayana (Tantric) Buddhism, introduced to Tibet in the ninth century by Guru Rimpoche, and in Khumbu much later. When Guru Rimpoche, the great "lotus born" Indian saint known in Sanskrit as Padmasambhava, came to Tibet and Khumbu, he battled the wrathful *srungma* mountain gods of the Bön religion and subdued them, turning them into defenders of the Buddhist faith. They now reside on the region's five

Sherpas work diligently to prepare their fields for planting.

great mountains, surrounded by other deities such as the protector god Khumbu Yülha.

The Tengboche Lama recounts that Guru Rimpoche forecast that Tibet would be plagued by wars and that devout people would have to flee to sacred Himalayan valleys of refuge known as *bé-yül*. Khumbu was one of four bé-yül that he identified, areas where mystical powers are concentrated and where spirits abound.

The patron saint of Khumbu, born about 350 years ago, announced that important gompas, celibate monasteries, would be built at some of these sites. Khumbu's first was built at Pangboche, but not until 1923 was the Tengboche monastery established by Lama Gulu. The gompas of Khumbu are now centers of learning and culture, and form the core of Sherpa spiritual life. The iconography of the gompas' lavish frescoes represents the Buddhist cosmos, replete with wrathful deities, wish-fulfilling gems, and flying horses bearing bodhisattvas across the heavens. Do these deities, demons, mythical places, and magical objects exist in physical form? Well, yes and no. All physical objects are impermanent and transitory, a creation of the mind, they say—and the mind itself is illusory, proved through Buddhist dialectics to have no inherent, independent existence. For the Sherpas, therefore, Mount Everest is a creation of mind over matter.

Mani stones line the trail up the beautiful Chhukung Valley in Sagarmatha National Park.

of Long Life), a line of monks playing instruments, the Lopon and his umbrella carrier, and finally patrons and important guests.

In a dozen dances, the colorfully robed and masked dancers depict, among other religious concepts, the conversion of pre-Buddhist demons into defenders of the Buddhist faith. Some dances illuminate the demons and obstacles that create afflictive emotions such as anger, jealousy, lust, and greed.

The monks' swirling and levitating motions are not merely theater. "Today, despite changes on every hand," Buddhist scholar Richard Kohn has pointed out, "lamas are still the heroes of the Everest region. The monks distribute magic pills to provide

sustenance and physical well-being to all who take them. The fearsome deities with whom the lama and monastery must deal are paraded before the public. The monks abandon their dull maroon uniforms and don the splendid brocades of tantric magicians, with *mudras* (mystical hand gestures) and magic weapons matching the chaotic forces of the supernatural, threat for threat."

Like any ritual, prayer, or teaching, Mani Rimdu ultimately intends to change the way people think or see, to impart a new vision and awareness. For outsiders as well as Sherpas, simply viewing the ceremony can bring merit, remove obstacles, and allow the fruits of its blessings to accrue.

A NATIONAL PARK

Before 1978, fewer than 3,000 tourists entered Khumbu each year, and most of them trekked to Everest Base Camp. By 2010 the number had grown to more than 25,000. The growth of trek tourism—and income for the Sherpas—has led to increased demand for resources, primarily wood for fuel and construction timber, and grass fodder for yaks.

In response to this, the government of Nepal in 1976 designated Khumbu as Sagarmatha National Park (SNP). The park borders the Makalu-Barun National Park and Conservation Area, to the east, and the massive Qomolangma Nature Preserve in Tibet, to the north—forming one of the largest blocks of contiguous protected area in Asia.

The Himalayan tahr, a species of wild goat, can be seen grazing above villages and beside trek routes, along with the rare and diminutive goral, a goat-antelope. Snow leopard sightings are rare, though Sherpa herders experience some leopard depredation on yaks in their high pastures.

The musk deer is more common. The male, as large as a medium-size dog, has two long, distinctive canine teeth. Within the park, musk deer are habituated to the proximity of humans, where predators don't often venture. But there is a flourishing market

Sagarmatha National Park provides shelter for rare animals like snow leopards and wild goats.

Himalayan tahr, listed as near threatened, linger under Lhotse.

for the male's musk pod, valued at several times the price of gold. As the species becomes scarcer outside the park, poachers have been lured inside its boundaries. They are often apprehended.

When SNP was created, it wasn't practical to curtail completely the residents' environmental impact. Park managers felt that if growth could be managed, the Sherpas' relatively sustainable, subsistence lifestyle might complement the park's biodiversity. But trees are being cut faster than they are growing.

More than all other uses of wood combined, burning it for cooking and heating is the most common. Each Sherpa hearth burns two to four metric tons of wood each year, and trekking lodges burn ten times this amount. In the 1950s and '60s, each expedition consumed more than seven metric tons of firewood. But in 1979, the park banned the sale of firewood to trekking groups and expeditions, and halted the burning of outdoor campfires. Expeditions and trekking groups are now

> "
>
> It's a region of astounding beauty, full of history and myth. I don't know any other mountain like it.
>
> ~KENTON COOL, IN MOUNTAIN HEROES: PORTRAITS OF ADVENTURE
>
> "

required to carry a quantity of kerosene or propane sufficient for the duration of their stay.

Conservation has deep roots among the Sherpas. The traditional, locally appointed forest guardians called *shingi-nawa* are one thriving local institution. From each village, Sherpas select two guardians who control the cutting of green wood for firewood, and villagers building a house must apply to them for roof beams and structural timbers. The shingi-nawa describe exactly where trees can be cut, usually not more than one in a given location.

In recent years, glacial melting has also become a concern. This melting has led to glacial lake outburst floods (GLOFs) that make the water supply unstable and impact the safety and livelihood of those who live in the region.

Thirty-five years ago, Khumbu had virtually no schools, medical care, or basic amenities such as drinking water systems and improved bridges. Sir Edmund Hillary, who devoted his life to helping the Sherpas of Solu-Khumbu District, knew that aid in the form of cash donations would do little to help. Since 1960, his Himalayan Trust has raised money for a large number of projects, all in response to requests by the Sherpas. From their experience as traders—for which math skills and the ability to draft business agreements are essential—Sherpa elders have long recognized the need for literacy.

"Our children have eyes, but still they are blind," one elder said years ago. This general sentiment prompted the construction of several primary schools and a high school in Khumbu villages.

When smallpox was ravaging the Indian subcontinent, the Himalayan Trust was able to immunize most of the people of Solu-Khumbu. Virtually all new cases of goiter and cretinism were eliminated as well, following an iodization campaign that accompanied the 1966 opening of the Khunde hospital. Still, illnesses are often blamed on the influence of ghosts, and many Sherpas consult shamans before going to the hospital—a place where wounds can be treated, but where people have been known to die.

ONWARD

Each day of the approach, David and Steve prepared storyboards and planned the day's film shooting, and David looked for images that would best capture Khumbu's 360-degree magnificence. Beyond Tengboche, they stopped on the Pangboche bridge, a suspended walkway 100 feet above the Imja Khola

river. From here they could see the double hump of Ama Dablam ("mother's amulet box"), and the distinctive hanging glacier below the summit.

During the test filming a year earlier, David had asked that he be lowered by a rope into the gorge with the IMAX camera. "The shots don't come to you," he said by way of explanation. "I envisioned filming while being suspended in space, a helicopter shot done with ropes."

Fifty feet downriver from the bridge, he located a good anchor on one side of the gorge. From a tree on the other side, the Sherpas threw across a rope, and David tied into it. They then lowered him using a system of belay devices, while lowering the camera alongside. Once in position, David took the camera off the belay, clipped it onto his belt, and sent the rope back up for the batteries and lenses.

(Continued on page 70)

In Sagarmatha National Park, a ghostly rhododendron forest thrives in the acidic soil of the Himalaya.

Across the gorge, more Sherpas on either side hauled on the slack rope, creating a V with David in the middle. "To get me at the right height," David recalled, "it needed to be a wide V, and took some tricky adjusting. If the rope was mismanaged, I would have swung like a pendulum and been smashed into the side of the gorge."

Yak drivers who were rounding the bend stopped when they reached the bridge, to let the yaks cross first. Yaks will spook if a load becomes snagged on the handrail or wire mesh of the bridge, and in their terror these huge animals have been known to injure themselves, and as a result also damage the bridge and their loads. David was especially concerned about the camera gear, having already chased a recalcitrant yak that had turned around and trotted down the valley with some IMAX camera equipment.

Jamling saw the gorge as a good place for prayer flags: The strong wind there would carry the prayers aloft. He unraveled a string of flags and strung it along the rail of the bridge. He had already left prayer flags at two other power spots along the approach route: above Namche Bazar and near the Dewoche nunnery. He would save the rest for the mountain, he decided.

Through the fog, the team hiked past simple stone houses, wind-stunted juniper, and more piles of mani stones. Beyond Pangboche, the vegetation gave way to rocks and lichens. Crossing a low pass within the valley, the Sherpas each selected rocks from beside the trail and placed them on a large cairn of stones, in thanks for the merit they would gain as pilgrims and for the good fortune of subsequent travelers.

> "
> I think **everybody has a place inside them that mountains can fill.** Mountains carry great respect with people around the world, so it doesn't surprise me at all that many people use mountains to find this. That's what I did, myself.
>
> ~NEAL BEIDLEMAN,
> IN *STORM OVER EVEREST*
> "

THE ROUTE TO BASE CAMP

On March 28, the expedition took a detour to the 14,300-foot yak pastures of Dingboche. For several days they camped next to herders' huts that had been converted into solar-powered lodges offering yak steaks, cinnamon rolls, and hot showers.

They filmed, washed clothes, and hiked to higher elevations to begin their acclimatization, the physiological process whereby the body's oxygen delivery system adjusts to the lower quantity of oxygen available in each breath. The more time spent at 14,000 feet, the better the team would be able to handle the two-day ascent to Base Camp, at 17,600 feet.

Ed, Jamling, and Jangbu had their hands full. Each load for Base Camp weighed about 66 pounds; yaks can carry two of these, but organizing a hundred yaks was a tall order. The cargo would have to be shuttled.

"It's not easy keeping track of 200 loads," Ed volunteered. "We haven't lost one yet, though at times they've been spread out over six villages." Ed consulted his list frequently, which seemed redundant considering his near perfect recall of the contents and location of each load.

Ed and Jamling went ahead to assess the condition of the trail. Yaks attempting to reach Base Camp had been postholing and bellying out in drifts of snow, especially on north-facing slopes. The Sherpas refused to lead the yaks beyond Lobuche, a day's walk below Base Camp. They can be tempted by hazard pay themselves, but they won't risk their yaks for any price. Ed and Jamling radioed to Jangbu to begin looking for porters.

The season's high snowfall, Ed felt, might at least make for better conditions on the mountain. Some of the rock would be covered with snow, making the

(previous spread) Sunrise spreads its fingers across the sacred Gokyo Lakes, a two-day walk from Namche Bazar.

TOURISM BRINGS DOLLARS AND CHANGE TO KHUMBU

In 1964, the year that Sir Edmund Hillary and anthropologist Jim Fisher worked alongside Sherpas to construct the airstrip at Lukla, 20 intrepid tourists visited Khumbu. No one foresaw that, within a few decades, Lukla would become a gateway into Khumbu for as many as 30,000 trekkers and climbers annually.

Now, nearly every Khumbu Sherpa is working in, or involved with, mountaineering or tourism. Jim Fisher believes that modern tourism is akin to the ancient tradition of pilgrimage, which for centuries has been an organized and commercial undertaking. Indeed, many tourists proudly identify themselves as pilgrims.

"Truth to tell," Fisher said, "Sherpas are mystified that Westerners spend so much time and money to see what to them are sometimes sacred but not very interesting mountains. Even the most experienced sirdars admit they cannot fathom why foreigners climb, although they have hunches about motives— principal among them fame, money, and science."

Dr. David Shlim noted some of the changes over three decades of working at the Himalayan Rescue Association Aid Post at Pheriche. "My wife, four-year-old son, and I sat at some outdoor tables at the edge of Khumjung, Ama Dablam massively at our backs, sipping cappuccino and eating fresh-baked pizzas from a large electric oven. It was different from sharing boiled potatoes around the hearth of a Sherpa home, but it was hard to say it was less pleasant."

"The new breed of Sherpas no longer wear sheepskin pants," Jim Fisher said, "but they know who they are. True, they wear down jackets, drink sugar (instead of salt) tea, and partition their homes into smaller rooms that are easier to heat, but these are superficial matters in themselves.

1996: **The proprietress of a trekking lodge where the** *Everest* **team found sustenance in Khumbu**

What is more important is that Sherpas are proud of being Sherpas and Buddhists."

Education has played a role in the Sherpas' monumental socioeconomic ascendancy. In 1961, Hillary's Himalayan Trust established Khumbu's first high school, in Khumjung. One young student, Ang Zangbu, carried loads barefoot for years to pay for schoolbooks and lodging. He became a jet airliner pilot at the age of 27. And Sherpa doctors trained in the West are now stationed at two area hospitals. The environment and culture have benefited from education, as well. Some have taken training as park managers and anthropologists.

Sherpa and foreign observers are concerned that some of the larger changes aren't coming from tourism, but from Sherpa increasingly living their lives in Kathmandu and abroad. Many Khumbu children don't learn the Sherpa language and can't imagine living full-time in their parents' homeland. The United States offers the most attractive opportunities, and many Khumbu Sherpas can be found there—having leap-frogged over Malaysia and the Middle East, the migratory labor destinations for as many as 1,500 Nepalis each day.

Of the Sherpas who return to Nepal, and of those who remained, many are investing their foreign income and local tourism earnings in their traditions and homeland. Meanwhile, those with larger business and political motivations face the prism of a Hindu-majority political system diffracted into a rainbow of political parties. But no challenge is insurmountable, it seems, for the widely traveled Khumbu Sherpa. Along the way, they have mastered what has been called Nepal's three major religions: Hinduism, Buddhism, and tourism.

climbing less technical. But the team remembered the tragic avalanches that killed more than 60 people the previous November, after a cyclone in the Bay of Bengal veered north to the Himalaya. Trekking guide Brian Weirum reported that the nearby valley of Gokyo, a picturesque trekkers' destination known for its turquoise lakes and staggering views, received over ten feet of snowfall in 36 hours. There, a wet snow avalanche buried a yak herder's teahouse, killing 26 people, including 13 trekkers and their Sherpa guides and kitchen crew. Across the width of the country, more than 500 stranded people were rescued by helicopter.

A SACRED SITE

En route to Lobuche, above the hamlet of Duglha, the team rested at a place called Chukpö Laré, the site of a number of large stone cairns erected by the Sherpas. Chukpö Laré is referred to as a memorial site, but it is primarily a place of ceremony and ritual. If a Sherpa dies at Base Camp or on the mountain and his body is recovered, it is brought to Chukpö Laré for cremation.

Most of the expedition's Sherpas had relatives who were cremated or honored here, and they all stopped to recite a prayer for their benefit. Jamling visited each of the more than 30 *chö-lung* monuments, and prayed and chanted. He stayed longer than the others.

"While returning from the summit in 1993, my cousin Lobsang Tshering Bhutia fell to his death.

> 66
> Mountains are not fair or unfair, **they are just dangerous.**
>
> ~REINHOLD MESSNER
> 99

We're unsure of what happened, but he may have run out of oxygen and become delirious. Team members carried his body down here and cremated him."

Corpses are not empty vessels, at least not immediately, and a form of the deceased's spirit may continue to reside within the body, Sherpas believe. Thus it is best for one's reincarnation if lamas can be present to perform the proper rituals. The bodies left on the mountain create a special problem: Without funerary rites, malevolent spirits can linger in their vicinity and cause harm. Devout Buddhists, however, say that people with pure motivation will be little troubled by these wandering souls.

If possible, lamas officiate at the cremation, and they treat the fleshly body as a sacred offering; it is first purified, then given by fire. In a similar ceremony on the north side of Everest, dead Tibetans are flayed and left for consumption by vultures in what is known as "sky burial."

In the deceased Sherpa's home village, wealthy families will light 100,000 butter lamps in their private chapels and in the monastery, in an appeal for a favorable reincarnation. Monks are called to the Sherpa's home, too, and the soul is prepared for travel through the transitory, after-death state of *bardo*. On the 49th day after death, the person is reincarnated.

The ashes are then molded into clay votive tablets called *tsa-war*, which are returned to the memorial site and placed inside the chö-lung monuments. Sacred objects are enclosed with them, including a

FLASH FORWARD JAMLING TENZING NORGAY

I n 2001, Norgay wrote a memoir called *Touching My Father's Soul* about his experience climbing Everest. In 2002, he and Peter Hillary (Edmund Hillary's son) were part of an Everest expedition meant to commemorate the 50th anniversary of their fathers' first ascent. Norgay runs an adventure and travel company, Tenzing Norgay Adventures, which offers expeditions in and around the Himalaya. In 2012, Norgay and his siblings started the Tenzing Norgay Sherpa Foundation to help the Sherpa of the Himalaya. As a motivational speaker, he often talks about his climbing experiences.

Sherpas lugged gear and supplies to Everest Base Camp for the American expedition in 1963.

piece of juniper with carved inscriptions that must be oriented in the precise alignment it had as part of the standing tree, which is labeled before felling.

Ultimately, the chö-lung represent aspirations for a permanent state of peacefulness—of nirvana. Prayers recited here are said for all sentient beings. "In death, humans lose their individuality," Jamling explained. "That's why we discourage keeping souvenirs or remembrances of the dead, and names are not inscribed here."

Chukpö Laré is not an ancient site. In 1970, after six Sherpas were killed by an avalanche during a large Japanese expedition, the Incarnate Lama of Tengboche hiked up and sanctified the area. It is distinguished from other funeral sites in that the

Sherpas cremated here all died untimely deaths, from unnatural causes. This complicates reincarnation and is difficult to resolve ritually.

Audrey Salkeld stresses that Sherpas have paid a disproportionately high price in lives lost on Everest. In the first 70 years of Everest climbing, 54 Nepali and Indian Sherpas were killed—more than a third of the total climbing deaths in that period. In 2014, 17 climbing Sherpas were killed when a chunk of ice broke off the Khumbu Icefall. It was one of the worst climbing accidents in the mountain's history.

Because of their contribution to route fixing and ferrying supplies, especially in the Khumbu Icefall, Sherpas are exposed to riskier parts of the mountain than their employers. Until recently, the

73

sirdar's agency was required to carry a $5,000 life insurance policy for every Sherpa who entered the Icefall. Things are changing in the aftermath of the tragic 2014 avalanche, bringing that number to around $11,000. Many are saying it should be much higher.

PORTERS TO BASE CAMP

When the yaks arrived at Lobuche, at 16,168 feet, the Sherpas unloaded them and joined the team members in sorting boxes and duffels for portering. Everyone was coughing and red-faced; even the veteran climbers weren't accustomed yet to the cold and altitude.

Porters were hard to find. Above the last villages it is difficult to recruit them in the best of conditions, and the high demand from all the expeditions had quickly led to astronomical pricing. But no challenge was too big for Jangbu. His perpetual grin, as deferential as it was devilish, betrayed a keen business sense. He had been issued a bright yellow walkie-talkie, and made sure he talked into it importantly when passing through villages and around young Sherpa women. He wasn't going to let the loads be delayed.

From Lobuche, Base Camp was no easy jaunt. Many trekkers never reach it, and Steve briefly suspected that his light-headedness from hypoxia—the shortfall in oxygen resulting from reduced atmospheric pressure at higher altitudes—might keep him from getting there. "The trail seemed to change form," he said, "and my feet became disembodied appendages that found each step as if on their own." Robert stopped and threw Steve's pack on top of his, and watched him for any signs of his hypoxia progressing into altitude sickness.

As usual, Araceli sang to herself as she walked with the rhythmic, buoyant energy of someone who might break into dance at any moment.

1996: **Yaks usually never break their stride in the upper Khumbu, but deep snows kept them from reaching Base Camp.**

CHAPTER THREE

AT HOME
ON THE GLACIER

"Changba, the head cook, stood waiting outside the kitchen tent—a tray filled with cups of tea in one hand and a gallant welcome wave in the other," reported Liesl Clark, describing the team's April 3 arrival at Base Camp. "The terrain here is otherworldly, with ice spires and shiny blue pinnacles. The rocks—which Roger Bilham informs us are a combination of granite and migmatite—look clean and regular, like Hollywood props jumbled into chaotic piles."

Two weeks on the trail were over. The Sherpa support staff had arrived at Base Camp a few days ahead of the others, and had carved out tent sites from the clutter of ice and rock on the margin of the glacier. Much additional work would be needed to prepare their home for the next two months. A winding line of porters from ethnic groups with names like Rai, Limbu, and Tamang worked its way toward camp.

As the loads came in, the Sherpas checked off their numbers. Jamling directed them onward: sacks of grain, fresh vegetables, and cans of kerosene to the kitchen tent; other food and climbing hardware to the storage tent (referred to as the 7-Eleven); film equipment to the camera tent; the satellite phone, computers, and printers to the "communications corner" of the dining tent. "If you can break it

Crossing ladders slung across crevasses at Base Camp takes practice and a dose of daring.

down small enough to carry it, you'll probably find it here," summarized production manager Liz Cohen. She had her hands full keeping track of the finances, media, shot lists, and communication with the outside world.

Both the climbing and film teams were unacclimatized to the 17,600-foot elevation. "Just existing is an effort," Roger explained. "While sitting, you feel relatively normal . . . but then stand up . . . and you can't form a sentence . . . of more than four words or so . . . because you're breathing so hard."

Beyond camp was the dreaded Icefall—the Khumbu Glacier's tongue of unstable ice that rudely protrudes from the valley between Nuptse and Everest. David and the climbers stood eyeing the treacherous Icefall, wondering quietly about the condition of this year's route through it.

The amphitheater of mountains surrounding Base Camp echoed the sounds of rumbling, billowing avalanches. Huge chunks of ice would tear off the Lho La, the wall that leads to the base of Everest's West Ridge, and come crashing down with thunderous roars. "Lying in our tents at night, it sounded like the *1812 Overture*," Audrey Salkeld recalled.

The sound and motion swelled beneath them, too; Base Camp is situated on the edge of the glacier itself. "The Khumbu glacier is ice under stress: creaking and bumping and clicking and snapping

> 66
> My very first view of Everest, it was **a long moment and a big hard swallow** and the thought was: 'I'm not so sure whether I can do this.'
> ~LOU KASISCHKE, IN
> *STORM OVER EVEREST*
> 99

and cracking and squeaking—a constant babble," Roger said. "It's always reminding us that we're camping on a dynamic sheet of ice."

Just as dynamic are the flocks of yellow-billed choughs, soaring on updrafts, their movements matching the playfulness of the wind itself. They've been seen poking about the South Col, at 26,000 feet, along with another Base Camp denizen, *gorak*—ravens—which have cadged food even higher. Gorak, the Sherpas say, can be messengers of the deceased and bearers of their souls.

HIGH-ALTITUDE CUISINE

Each morning, Changba woke before sunrise to prepare the first of endless rounds of tea, which he delivered to the tents amid clouds of steam and hearty good mornings. All the while, he carried on in cheerful song, the lyrics alive with the joy and angst of mountain life.

Audrey found her spot in the kitchen and filed her second report to MacGillivray Freeman Films and the *NOVA* Web site:

"Base Camp is now quite a city . . . It is curious that, having voluntarily removed ourselves as far as possible from the trappings of so-called civilization, expeditions then appear to vie with one another in creating alternative civilizations of ingenious comfort and complexity. Elaborate mess tents have sprung up, with electric lighting and in some cases heating, music, and comfy chairs and tables. Even the Sherpas compete in the construction

---

FLASH FORWARD **ROBERT SCHAUER**

Schauer has continued to climb and to film around high mountains. In 2000, he worked as a cameraman with David Breashears on the IMAX film *Kilimanjaro: To the Roof of Africa*. He returned and summited Everest once again in 2004, while working on David Breashears's documentary *Storm Over Everest*. He is the founding director of the international film festival Mountainfilm, which takes place annually in Graz, Austria. Though he officially ended his climbing career in 2006, he returned to Kilimanjaro in 2014 and climbed it a second time.

of impressive camp kitchens, mostly *sangars* (dry stone walls) with pitched roofs made from heavy-duty tarpaulins and laid out inside with all the economy and efficiency of kitchens in the best hotels."

The kerosene and propane stoves were always going, and the climbers and film team hung out in the kitchen for warmth. Sherpas visited from other camps, and the Sherpa women who came up with loads laughed and joked constantly. The Sherpas invited the porters in and fed them—then put them to work out back, doing the dishes.

The shelves on one wall of the kitchen tent were weighted with cans and boxes, and a leg of yak hung from the crossbeam. Araceli's mother had sent her off with a large ham, as she had for each of her daughter's Himalayan expeditions.

"I brought something very tasty, too," Robert said in his Austrian German accent. He waited for Araceli to respond.

"*Zumzing*? So what does *zumzing* taste like?" Araceli teased, her attempt at a German accent enhanced with a Catalan inflection. Robert showed her his large wrapped *speck*, a smoked ham from Austria "loaded with valuable calories." To wash it down, he had packed alongside it a liter of Voglbeer schnapps. Robert proudly told her that the Voglbeer bush, which grows at tree line near his home, supplies the fruit for this distillate. "I want to see you after you have drunk all of that and are destroyed," Araceli gibed.

Jamling had brought his own specialty: four kilograms of *tsampa*, which he would take to the higher camps. This roasted barley flour digests easily and provides lasting fuel, though a handful of dry flour can be hard for the uninitiated to get down. Some Sherpas carry a small leather sack in which they mix tsampa, tea, butter, and sugar, and knead them into dough balls called *pak*. Nuts and other ingredients are sometimes added to form a Sherpa version of an energy bar.

On April 10, Paula, Sumiyo, and Changba prepared a full Japanese dinner, but most meals were not so lavish, consisting of creatively disguised cooked potatoes. One afternoon when Ed returned from a load carry to Camp I, he was sorting loads for Camps I and II. "How about Spam tonight, and maybe some wine?" he queried toward the kitchen tent.

"Spam?" Sumiyo said quizzically. Ed nodded enthusiastically to her, then handed a roll of duct tape to a climbing Sherpa who was repairing his snow gaiters.

Preparing food for teams at Base Camp is a ceaseless endeavor.

"Spam," Sumiyo repeated. Pondering intently, she enunciated aloud to herself the other English words she had been practicing. "Revision . . . Tremendous . . . Awesome . . . Spam."

Araceli perked up. "Did someone say 'Spam?' I'm ongry."

"Are you *angry* that we have Spam, or are you *hungry* to have some?" Ed asked her, provoking boisterous laughter from the crew in the kitchen.

"No, *ongry*," Araceli repeated indignantly, unfazed by the laughter. "I want some food, of course, like I do always."

"I think you get *angry* when you get *hungry*," Ed joked. Araceli flashed a brief smile, then swatted him. A party of rose finches abandoned their foraging for scraps and fluttered off.

Each night Jamling would check out what the Westerners had cooked and then what the Sherpas had prepared, before choosing where to eat. A sip of wine would be hard to pass up, he decided.

Evening dinner dress consisted of a down parka, hat, and gloves—donned each afternoon during "down up time," the moment the sun went over the ridge. Base Camp visitors noticed that the dining room was as cold as a meat locker, but hunger made the food delicious. After dinner, team members stumbled through the dark to their tents. Despite the cold, porters stood around in the evenings in rubber flip-flop sandals without socks, swearing that they felt fine.

"We're on our honeymoon here," Ed said. "Living dormitory style we don't really have a chance for privacy, but I'd rather have Paula on this trip than write letters to her."

The 1963 American expedition to Everest put six men on the 29,035-foot summit, one pair laboring up the unconquered West Ridge while the others took the South Col route (red) pioneered by Hillary and Norgay a decade earlier. Sherpas and climbers leap-frogged supplies up the forbidding slopes through a series of camps placed a day's climb apart. The 1996 ascent by the *Everest* IMAX film team also headed up the South Col, but pitched one less campsite, electing to "sprint" from Camp IV to the top and back in an 18-hour marathon climb.

Northeast Ridge

Bei Peak
24,878 ft
7,583 m

Khumbutse
21,867 ft
6,665 m

Rongbuk
Glacier

Lho La

Lingtren
22,142 ft
6,749 m

Pumori
23,507 ft
7,165 m

Khumbu Gla

Icef

Base Camp
17,600 ft
5,364 m

Kh

— 1996 *Everest* Expedition,
South Col Route

✳ The earthquake of
April 25, 2015, may
result in a small change
in the height of Everest,
but that measurement
was not finalized at the
time of printing.

complex camera gear—film and magazines, filters, from Brad, who was responsible for overseeing the preparation required long hours back safely. The preparation required long hours a properly functioning camera to the summit—and Robert, and David, each of them dedicated to getting a symbiotic rapport with Steve, he had developed a symbiotic rapport with Steve, have jungles and warm water," he explained. But southern California, and most of my favorite places time to adjust to glacier life. "I live on the beach in

It took filmmaker Brad Ohlund a little more found in the Asan Tol bazaar.

with limited resources—I love it!" Already he had fashioned a voltage transformer from parts he had been mending the electronic and solar gadgets that inevitably break, while working in tiny, cold corners "Since we arrived," Roger reported cheerfully, "I've

Within a week the team had regained some strength.

GLACIER GADGETS

matte boxes, battery packs, shades, tripods, countless accessories, and the unwieldy camera body itself.

The fax machine and satellite phone drew more juice than the jury-rigged solar system could provide, and the generator was frequently needed as a backup. In the minus 16°F mornings, starting it required a hundred pulls on the cord and a magical blend of adjustments to the choke and throttle.

The "sat" phone did get some use. On April 15, Dr. Charles Warren, one of the few surviving prewar Everesters, was delighted to receive a call from Audrey and the team, wishing him a happy 90th birthday. A member of the '35, '36, and '38 expeditions, Warren discovered the body of Maurice Wilson, the eccentric pilot who in 1934 hoped to reach the summit through fasting and prayer. Warren and his companions committed the remains of "the Mad Yorkshireman," as the press dubbed him, to a

1996: An avalanche booms and billows down from the Lho La within sight of Base Camp.

crevasse below the ice chimney of the North Col. They then sat beneath an overhang and opened his diary, which made for eerie reading.

The chat with Warren launched Audrey into after-dinner stories, and she spoke of the film that she and David had scripted and produced on the fate of George Mallory and Andrew Irvine, the two British climbers who disappeared high on Everest in 1924. In her blue Volkswagen bug, David and Audrey crisscrossed England seeking out other veterans of early Everest attempts. They first visited Captain John Noel, photographer and filmmaker for the 1922 and 1924 expeditions, in his weatherboard cottage on Romney Marsh in Kent. Noel had been an artillery instructor during the Great War, and he advised David to launch a succession of small "eggshell" bombs high on Everest to excavate the ice and snow, in the hope of finding traces of the two men. Then they motored to Cambridge to interview another nonagenarian, Professor Noel Odell, the last person to see Mallory and Irvine alive. In Bakewell, Sir Jack Longland described how, in 1933, his team had discovered an ice ax high on the mountain, which could only have belonged to one of the missing men.

Conrad Anker found Mallory's body in 1999, but no one has been able to locate Irvine or their camera. If the camera is found, it might contain film that—preserved by the cold—could be developed. If they had reached the summit, it is inconceivable that there would not be a summit shot to prove it.

Ed spoke unequivocally. "Even if Mallory and Irvine touched the summit, they didn't *make* it—that's like swimming to

> **"**
> When people think of mountains, **they think of Everest.** It's the highest mountain in the world and it's become its own identity—in and of itself—aside from any of the climbing that is done on it.
>
> ~DAVE MORTON,
> IN "THE STATE
> OF EVEREST"
> **"**

the middle of the ocean," he asserted. Sir Edmund Hillary was of the same opinion. "The point of climbing Everest," he said, "should not be just to reach the summit. I'm rather inclined to think that maybe it's quite important, the getting down."

CROWDING IN THE MIDDLE OF NOWHERE

By mid-April, Everest Base Camp had filled with 14 expeditions, and their camps stretched for a mile along the rumpled edge of the glacier. The climbers, Sherpas, Base Camp staff, and government liaison officers brought the Base Camp population to more than 300.

Araceli, accustomed to climbing in small parties on remote routes, was feeling crowded. "The approach to here has become commercial—you can even find sneakers to eat, just two hours from Base Camp! . . . I mean *Snickers*, the chocolate, not the shoes!" She laughed and drew a line around her

Members of the 1953 British expedition gather at Base Camp.

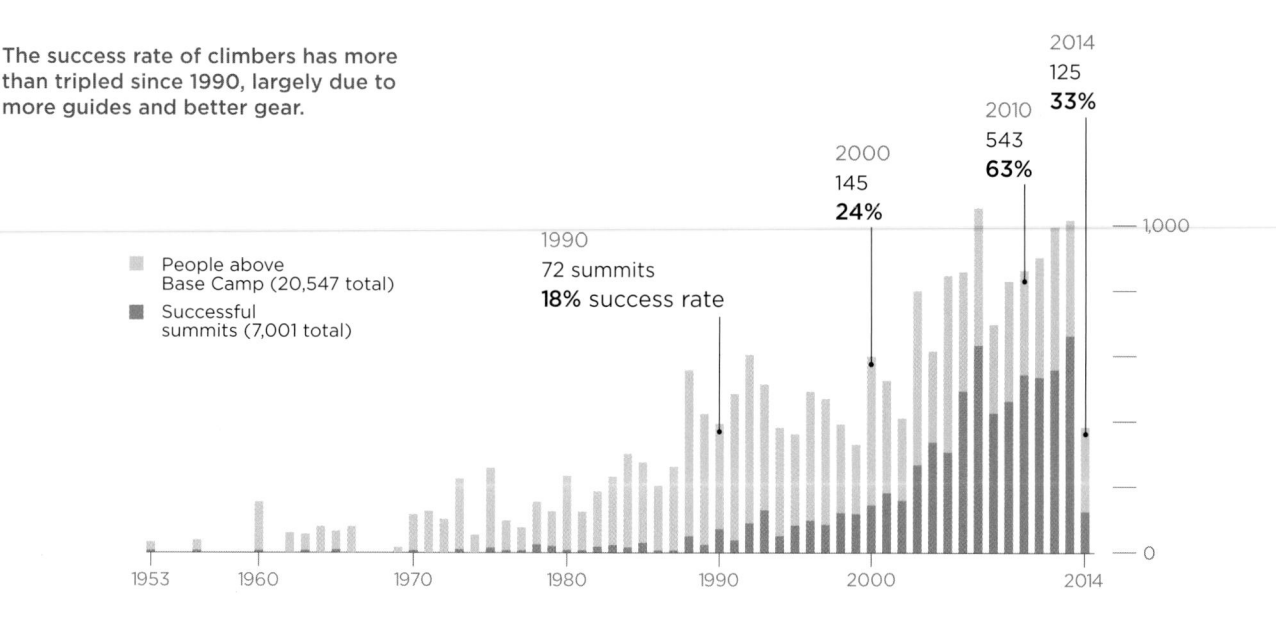

The success rate of climbers has more than tripled since 1990, largely due to more guides and better gear.

People above Base Camp (20,547 total)

Successful summits (7,001 total)

2014
125
33%

2010
543
63%

2000
145
24%

1990
72 summits
18% success rate

— 1,000

— 0

1953   1960   1970   1980   1990   2000   2014

mouth to show where the chocolate usually becomes smeared. "Oh, and you can find the shoes, too."

Many of the leaders of these expeditions—David Breashears, Scott Fischer, Rob Hall, Todd Burleson, Pete Athans, and Henry Todd—were eminences in the world of guided climbing, and all were friends. Nonetheless, Base Camp hummed with an undercurrent of competition between the groups. To make a living climbing, one must be known and recognized. This recognition is achieved mainly by assembling a portfolio of successfully climbed peaks. It is to the guide's advantage, professionally, to excel where others haven't. Rivalry could be expected.

This year, Scott Fischer's and Rob Hall's expeditions were the largest. Fischer's Mountain Madness camp displayed banners advertising Starbucks coffee, and Sherpas painted "New Zealand camp" in large letters on a glacial boulder at Hall's campsite.

Scott Fischer moved about Base Camp informally, and his warmth and positive approach infected

> 66
> Attempting to climb Everest **affects people strongly,** and seems to initiate fundamental changes that set them on **unexpected paths.**
>
> ~RESEARCHER AT
> THE INSTITUTE
> OF PERSONALITY
> ASSESSMENT AND
> RESEARCH
> 99

everyone he met. Ed had climbed K2 with Fischer in '92, and Scott had photographed Ed and Paula's wedding, only a few weeks earlier. "Scott is freewheeling and almost casual about organization," Ed said. "He assumes that the details—how much fuel or how many ropes are needed—will fall into place, and for him they usually do. 'Forge ahead! We're going for it!' is his motto. He's fun and inspiring, overflowing with energy and enthusiasm. But sometimes I feel he could use some reining in."

Ed described Hall as the exact opposite: calculating, meticulous, and organized. "Rob is always assessing conditions, the weather, what the clients are doing, asking himself *'what if?'* He uses his incredible drive to help people achieve their dreams, and takes joy in a task well done."

Ed respected Hall for his climbing expertise and experience, and Scott Fischer was planning to join the two of them on a climb of Manaslu immediately *(Continued on page 88)*

IMAXING THE MOUNTAIN

"Everyone told me the IMAX camera was too big and heavy to take to the top of Mount Everest, that it was an impossible goal," said producer and director Greg MacGillivray. "But I was steadfast. We had to shoot the summit with full IMAX images. Those shots were the key to the entire film."

MacGillivray went to the best technicians at IMAX Corporation's engineering department to design a new camera. For more than a year, Kevin Kowalchuk and Gord Harris worked to build a lighter camera that was small enough for the Sherpas to carry all the way to the top of the mountain and that would withstand Everest's harsh conditions. David Breashears laid out the specifications:

• The weight of the camera body could not exceed 26 pounds.

• The camera would have to withstand minus 40°F temperatures for 24 hours and then operate reliably with the flip of a switch.

• Large, accessible knobs and lens mounts would be needed to allow an exhausted camera operator to film with potentially impaired motor and thinking skills.

At IMAX Corporation headquarters in Toronto, the engineering team began with an IMAX Mark II camera model, modified the lightweight and durable magnesium body, then simplified the electronics and removed the eight-pound flywheel.

"We turned a '96 Chevy into a '56 Chevy," said cameraman and technical supervisor Brad Ohlund, "while reducing its weight by half." At exactly 25 pounds, the Everest model weighed in at less than half the Mark II's normal weight.

Extreme cold congeals lubricants and makes film brittle, so the engineers built in a hand crank for loosening up the system and used a lubricant that remains viscous down to minus 100°F. Conventional batteries fail in the extreme cold, and so the camera needed to be powered by a nonrechargeable lithium battery pack.

When fully loaded with lens and 500-foot film magazine, the camera package weighed in at 48 pounds. After testing the camera system in a blizzard on a New Hampshire mountaintop, IMAX rented a cold test chamber used by the defense industry to put the camera through its paces.

"When we stepped in, it was minus 50°F," Breashears said, "giving us an opportunity to test our expedition's down clothing, too, which we were wearing." They loaded film barehanded, plugged in the battery, and turned the camera on. "It performed flawlessly every time. That was the first moment I thought to myself: *We can really do this.*"

In 1995, MacGillivray sent Breashears and Kowalchuk to field-test the camera in Nepal. With 40 porters they trekked over 160 miles, ascending and descending more than 80,000 vertical feet. They left the camera outside overnight, on rocky outcrops, with only a nylon cover for protection. "In the mornings, I'd turn the camera on," Breashears said. "In 27 days not a single scene was lost to camera or battery malfunction."

But the 1996 film expedition was not without its technical challenges. In one nerve-racking incident, the IMAX camera broke down on the mountain. "At Base Camp, Brad Ohlund worked 48 hours straight to get it repaired and running again for the team on the mountain," said MacGillivray. "But at the summit, the camera worked perfectly. Our team got three minutes of historic images, and I used every second in the film."

The IMAX camera had to perform, even in the bitter cold.

The warm sunset glow that sometimes bathes the slopes of Everest makes the mountain seem deceptively calm.

following Everest. Ed had guided several commercial climbs for Hall's New Zealand company, Adventure Consultants, and he anticipated a long-lasting partnership.

Climbers and clients this year had come to Everest with a variety of motives, not all of them clear.

"Egos and other factors are at work here," Paula said, voicing a concern that Ed had shared earlier. "People can become selfish on the mountain, and lose sight of what's important." Veteran climbers worry that many clients regard an attempt on Everest as a once-in-a-lifetime chance—predisposing

(previous spread) Headlamp trails look like fireflies as climbers weave through the bustling tents at Base Camp.

them to push their luck and take risks, without the experience that would help them gauge those risks. Out of seven Everest expeditions, Ed had summited three times. Most other experienced guides have even lower summit-to-attempt ratios. Nonetheless, during the approach to the mountain, Scott Fischer expressed a modern and not uncommon sentiment about Everest: "I mean, honestly speaking, we have learned how to climb Mount Everest, and are building the yellow brick road to the top."

It was a road that didn't require a driver's license. The Taiwanese team in particular was under-experienced, though it would be hard to fault them for trying. Audrey Salkeld noted that several of the Taiwanese had lost fingers to frostbite on previous climbs. "Imagine gaining your experience for Everest in a country as flat and warm as Taiwan," David said, adding that the Taiwanese climbers reminded him of Mallory and Irvine: sporting and eager, but poorly equipped—and in over their heads.

The most unusual approach was being made by a lone Swede, 29 years old, named Göran Kropp. Remarkably, Kropp had bicycled from Sweden to Nepal with most of his gear, and he intended to solo Everest in the purest sense of soloing—he would accept no help, not even a cup of tea, from others on the mountain. He was hauling his own supplies through the Khumbu Icefall on a route he had found himself.

> 66
> To struggle and to understand. Never the last without the first. **That is the law.**
> ~GEORGE MALLORY, IN *MOUNTAIN HEROES: PORTRAITS OF ADVENTURE*
> 99

MINDFULNESS

Jamling stood quietly studying the sprawling, impromptu tent city. He spoke with Wongchu about Geshé Rimpoche's lesson to him on Right Motivation. Just that day, Wongchu had lined up a group of young, playfully rebellious Base Camp support Sherpas. He lectured that he would fine them 10,000 rupees each if they didn't cooperate with Changba, if they weren't helpful to the team, or if they were involved in any extramarital sex at Base Camp. The Sherpas knew well that the last would offend the deities. Wongchu was especially concerned that any activity that generated emotions such as anger, jealousy, lust, or pride be avoided when on the

Scott Fischer's infectious enthusiasm and positivity often served him well as a climbing guide.

mountain, for these would affect one's mindfulness when climbing.

"Which flag should we fly, were we to fly one?" Robert mused at dinner one night.

Jamling pulled out the string of flags he intended to display on the summit: Nepal, India, Tibet, U.S.A., and the United Nations.

"My parents are from Tibet, but lived for long periods in Nepal and India, where I was raised. I studied and worked for years in the United States. The UN flag might represent me best—and our team as well. Look at us here." He nodded and looked around the dining tent. "Most of us are from different countries."

He gently passed his hand over another multicolored bundle and carefully untied it. "The most meaningful flag for me is this *lungta*, the prayer flag. Lungta is actually a 'wind horse' that bears a deity carrying wish-fulfilling gems, and their image is printed on many of the flags. But lungta also represents the degree of positive spiritual energy and awareness that propels a person—it's their level of divine inner support."

The Sherpa say that if their lungta is high, they will survive most any difficult situation, and if it is low, they can die even while sitting at home. A former Tengboche monk now working in the United States described the relationship between lungta and good luck as similar to that between principal and interest. "Cultivating one's lungta, through meditation and

> ❝
> **Mountaineering should be passion.** Not just to go home and say, 'Well, I've climbed Mount Everest.' It's absurd.
>
> ~NORMAN DYHRENFURTH, IN "THE STATE OF EVEREST"
> ❞

right actions, helps generate clear thinking," Jamling counseled.

He pulled out the other items he hoped to place on the summit: pictures of his mother and father, neatly framed in a red vinyl wallet; a photo of His Holiness the Dalai Lama; and an elephant-shaped rattle that his infant daughter selected from a pile of toys—perhaps significant in light of the Rongbuk lama's translation of "Chomolungma": Great Elephant Woman. Tenzing Norgay had also taken a small toy to the summit, selected for him by Jamling's sister.

"If we go for the top on the 9th of May, I feel that my father's spirit will be with us. That's the tenth anniversary of his death," Jamling said.

"Jamling and I shared a tent," Roger said, "and one evening he lent me a signed edition of his father's book describing the first climb. I read it by flashlight as he recited his prayers. I asked him what he was praying for. He said, 'I pray for the safety of all, and that I am worthy to follow in my father's footsteps.' It brought tears to my eyes. I always looked forward to chatting with Jamling, because our conversations always went slightly beyond the present; they were philosophical, never involving any shared experience."

PUJA AT BASE CAMP

Sherpas and climbers normally won't climb above Base Camp until the puja ceremony of purification

---

FLASH FORWARD   JON KRAKAUER

After returning from Everest in 1996, Krakauer wrote a narrative of the experience for *Outside* magazine. He then wrote *Into Thin Air*, a book that went on to become a finalist for the Pulitzer Prize and a best seller. He founded the Everest '96 Memorial Fund at the Boulder Community Foundation, which contributes to charities such as the American Himalayan Foundation. He has gone on to publish more nonfiction books, including *Under the Banner of Heaven* (2003) and *Where Men Win Glory* (2009).

Lakpa Sherpa, co-owner of the Himalayan Ascent Expedition Company, takes a quiet moment.

and propitiation has been completed. Each expedition performs its own puja, and they begin by building a handsome chorten-like structure, about eight feet high, which becomes the heart of the *lhap-so*, the worship site. Wongchu selected an auspicious day from the Tibetan calendar, then summoned an elderly monk from Pangboche.

The Base Camp puja is commonly described as a request for permission to climb the mountain, and for protection and good weather. But its liturgical meaning is much more complex. It is a category of *serkim* ("golden drink offering") ritual: Before any new undertaking such as building a house or climbing a mountain, a lama engages the deities and asks for their understanding and toleration for those activities.

The morning of the puja, Sherpas and team members brought offerings—bread, rice, barley, and fancier items such as chocolate and whiskey—to the lhap-so. The lama sat, and two Sherpas poured him tea and made him comfortable. As he read prayers aloud, some of the congregation meditated and prayed, while others moved about informally, as one may at most Sherpa ceremonies.

The Sherpa believe that the gods will provide for climbers—or deliver bad luck—even without this ceremony. But like meditation, the ritual is a form of discipline that opens one to receive the wisdom of these gods, empowering the faithful to better recognize beneficial or ominous situations when they arise. The serkim effectively activates the levels of concentration and awareness that are needed to succeed.

Not only must the climbers and Sherpas be purified before setting foot on the mountain, so must their equipment. In one part of the ritual, Sherpas ignite juniper boughs next to the altar. The team and climbing Sherpas then pass their ropes, crampons, ice axes, and other gear through the smoke, bathing it in protective wafts of incense. In the same way that the sweet smell of the juniper incense expels odors, the smoke dispels pollution and clears the way for favorable events.

The lama distributed red blessing strings called *sungdi* (from *sung-dü*, protection knot), made of thin braided nylon. The team tied one sungdi onto every item of equipment, to be left on for the duration of the expedition. "We Sherpas believe that sungdi—like the *sungwa* amulets—help protect us from the harmful spirits and situations that can push us into a crevasse, off the edge of a narrow ridge, or into the path of an avalanche," said Jamling. "But we recognize that these alone are insufficient to save us, of course."

Two Sherpas erected a tall prayer-flag pole and secured it in a stone enclosure. Seven colorful strings of prayer flags radiated from the top of the pole, their ends anchored nearby. The Sherpas say that if a gorak, or native raven, lands on the juniper branch on top of the pole during the puja, the expedition will be successful. If the pole breaks or is taken down, bad luck will ensue.

To close the ceremony, everyone sang in unison in a gradually rising tone, *Swoooooo!*—Go up, may good fortune arise!—while slowly elevating right hands full of tsampa. Repeating this a third time, they launched the flour skyward. In a joyous, chaotic moment, all shouted "*Lha gyalo!*—May the gods be victorious!"—and rubbed the flour in one another's

> 66
>
> If Everest can still be that mountain that inspires exploration, it serves something to the **greater direction of humanity**—because we are explorers as humans.
>
> ~CONRAD ANKER,
> IN "THE STATE
> OF EVEREST"
>
> 99

hair and on their cheeks to signify that they wished to live until their hair and beards turned white.

The lama poured chang as a communion. Jamling accepted some in his right hand, his left held respectfully beneath it. He drank a sip, then ran the rest through his hair to fully incorporate the blessing.

The climbers followed, and the offerings were passed out. "We all accepted some of the offerings, careful not to take too much," David said.

"You must not argue on this day," Wongchu cautioned. They didn't look as if they would: Everyone had begun dancing and drinking—in moderation.

CHECKING THE OXYGEN

Geshé Rimpoche's lesson on mindfulness called for attention to every safeguard. David inspected each of the team's 75 oxygen bottles and every regulator before sending them through the Icefall. The bottles were a lifeline, a ticket home. "We'll be very exposed above the South Col, where it's like being on the moon," he said, referring to the low atmospheric pressure—and likely to hypoxia, which imparts the sensation of not being fully earthbound. Though David expressed unease at the team's dependence on this technological crutch, he handled the bottles with a respect bordering on the religious.

In 1996, most climbers preferred the Poisk high-pressure oxygen system. Each of the Russian-made bottles weighs 6.6 pounds when full and provides six hours of oxygen flow at two liters per minute. The bottles are made of aluminum wrapped with strands of Kevlar, which help contain the 14,000 pounds of pressure. Though the Poisk system is still in use, some newly available oxygen systems—Top-out and Summit Oxygen—have started winning devotees on the mountain. They're lighter, which means they require less precious energy to carry.

1996: **In an enduring Base Camp tradition, climbing gear awaits a blessing at a lhap-so before climbers proceed.**

(Continued on page 97)

WHAT HAPPENS AT ALTITUDE?

It's a law of nature: Without oxygen, we die. At high altitude, oxygen is in short supply, and simply getting a good breath is a challenge to any climber.

Oxygen density at varying altitudes is a function of another basic law: gravity. Air has weight. At sea level it is compressed by the blanket of air above it, and is comfortably dense. At high altitudes, air pressure is lower and air is consequently thinner. Adjusting to reduced oxygen levels requires some rapid physiological changes and is followed by slower, long-term changes.

The first change is obvious. We breathe harder to get more oxygen into our lungs. Breathing harder provides the lungs with more oxygen, but also causes problems with loss of too much carbon dioxide. As a by-product of metabolism we need to exhale carbon dioxide, a swift and sensitive agent for adjusting the acidity of blood. Overbreathing "washes out" carbon dioxide, causing low acidity, or alkalosis—an abnormal condition that cannot be tolerated for long.

As we breathe faster and deeper, the heart also beats faster and harder, pumping more blood per beat and per minute. The small capillaries in tissues become more permeable when short of oxygen, causing fluid to leak into the tissues and concentrating the red blood cells, thereby increasing the blood's oxygen content.

These changes—increased breathing, higher output from the heart, and the concentration of blood—are "struggle responses." They protect the body from oxygen deprivation, or hypoxia, but they can't be sustained for long without provoking potentially life-threatening symptoms.

Given time, acclimatization is effective, but if we go too high too fast, the "struggle responses" may be inadequate and acclimatization too slow to provide us with enough oxygen, and we are likely to get "mountain sickness." Though we speak of several forms, they are all consequences of hypoxia.

Hypoxia can lead to acute mountain sickness, which in turn can develop into the more serious high-altitude pulmonary edema (HAPE), or even high-altitude cerebral edema (HACE), an early but ominous sign of a more serious brain disturbance caused by altitude. HACE can be difficult to recognize because it weakens the higher functions of the brain—judgment, perception, memory, and will.

EFFECTS OF HYPOXIA

Hypoxia: A condition in which the body as a whole or a region of the body is deprived of oxygen supply.

Low oxygen pressure at high altitude.

The carotid body, a cluster of specialized cells in the carotid artery, detects low oxygen levels in the blood and alerts the brain.

In response, the brain sends signals to the rest of the body to . . .

increase breathing rate and constrict vessels in the lungs

increase heart rate

dilate peripheral blood vessels in arms, legs, hands, and feet.

©2012 MAYO CLINIC

Physiologists continue to study the body's responses to extremes such as climbing Everest.

Except for Ed, who would be attempting to climb Everest a third time without bottled oxygen, the team would use oxygen when climbing above Camp III, at 24,000 feet. At Camp IV they planned to sleep with it on at a flow of about a half liter per minute. On summit day they would each consume three bottles.

WHAT OXYGEN DOES

Dr. Charles Houston, a pioneer of modern high-altitude physiology studies and an adviser on the film, would often explain that when working muscles don't receive enough oxygen, they can "go anaerobic" and begin burning fuel without oxygen. But this results in acidosis, which the body doesn't tolerate for long. Breathing bottled oxygen increases arterial oxygen and thereby hemoglobin saturation, which brings more oxygen to hungry tissues. And with more oxygen available, the extreme urge to breathe is reduced, giving both the feeling and reality of more energy.

Oxygen was first used in the 1920s, but with criticism from high-mountain purists—even though it was not clear at the time that climbing Everest without it would be possible. Until 1946, that is, when Houston oversaw Operation Everest, in which four human subjects in a decompression chamber were taken slowly (over a period of one month) to the decreased atmospheric pressure of Everest's "summit." There, two of the subjects were able to perform light work for a short period.

Houston pointed out that if Mount Everest, at 28 degrees north latitude, were located at the latitude of Alaska's Mount Denali, 63 degrees, it would have the barometric pressure of a peak at least another

Stephen Venables was 20 pounds lighter after climbing Everest.

500 feet higher—possibly making it unclimbable without bottled oxygen.

For emergencies, the team would have access to a novel item: an inflatable hyperbaric bag made of airtight reinforced vinyl, into which a very sick patient could be placed. It does the opposite of Houston's chamber: As the bag is continually pumped up by helpers, the air (and thus oxygen) pressure can be increased to that of lower altitudes. Afflicted climbers can improve their condition to the point where they are able to descend with minimal assistance.

(previous spread) 1996: Tossing offerings of barley flour, climbers and Sherpas conclude the puja ceremony.

ALTITUDE, SHERPAS, AND GEESE

Filmmaker Steve Judson sat on a rock one morning, a few days after arriving at Base Camp. "It's humbling, when I feel so bad, to watch the Sherpas scampering around as if they were at sea level." Aside from having had a longer opportunity for acclimatizing, many wonder if the Sherpa and other highland peoples are physiologically different from the rest of us. Physical anthropologist Dr. Cynthia Beall believes the Sherpa may possess a gene that allows more efficient oxygen delivery, giving them an advantage over lowlanders.

One part-time Himalayan resident, the bar-headed goose, is an even more remarkable acclimatizer

> "
> You feel like you're **one giant lung,** as if breathing is all there is to life.
> ~MICHAEL GROOM,
> CLIMBING GUIDE
> "

in this regard than the Sherpa or the Tibetan people. High-altitude physiologist Dr. Robert "Brownie" Schoene is impressed that these birds can "winter in the marshes of India, then—without the advantage of gradual acclimatization—get up and fly over the Himalaya to their summer breeding areas high on the Tibetan Plateau."

Like all birds, bar-headed geese have a remarkably efficient one-way flow of air into their lungs, which eliminates wasted breathing. But they also possess a hemoglobin molecule in the red blood cells that distinguishes them genetically from their lowland bird relatives. "This hemoglobin has a greater capacity for picking up oxygen in conditions of low oxygen pressure, and is able to unload that oxygen to the tissues that are starved for it," Schoene explained.

Thomas Jukes, a biologist who has studied bar-headed geese, suggests that one day Himalayan climbers might be able to receive transfusions of a similar, genetically engineered hemoglobin before ascending to high altitudes.

CAMP-BY-CAMP SIEGE

Most teams place their series of four mountain camps at locations that have been used for the past 40 years—sites that were initially selected for their relative safety from avalanche, rockfall, wind, and movement of the glacier. Each expedition groups its tents closely together, though these may be up to a few hundred yards from another expedition's camp.

After a route has been found through the Khumbu Icefall, the goal of every team is to establish and fully stock their four camps with supplies, so that the summit push can be made quickly from Base Camp or Camp II. This process generally takes a month or longer.

During the first week on the mountain, the Sherpas typically rise early, and in a couple of hours carry a 40- to 50-pound load to Camp I, at 19,500 feet, then return to Base Camp. When much of the gear

It is Sherpas who carry most of the supplies up to camps.

Sherpas' headlamps cut through the early morning dark as they carry loads through the Khumbu Icefall.

for the higher camps has been carried to Camp I, the gear is shuttled to Camp II, at 21,300 feet. There, the Sherpas set up a smaller version of Base Camp—Advance Base Camp, with a cook tent, dining tent, and individual tents. Most of the climbers' rest time above Base Camp is spent here. When acclimatized, they can climb directly from Base Camp to Camp II, and Camp I mainly becomes a way station for gear.

At Camp III, 24,000 feet, the climbers need only two tents; the Sherpas do not stay here, but generally go directly from II to IV.

Camp IV, the uppermost camp, is situated at 26,000 feet on the South Col, a broad saddle between Lhotse and Everest. The South Col is higher than all but 17 of the world's highest peaks, placing it in the "death zone," a poorly defined but easily recognized altitude

where climbers know they must limit their time as their condition deteriorates fairly quickly above this altitude. Here, six tents are erected, but until the night before the summit push, Camp IV is little more than a place to store oxygen and equipment.

The day before the summit attempt, the team climbs from Camp III to Camp IV, arriving there in the early afternoon. Here, they rest for a few hours and rehydrate themselves, or "brew up," before departing about midnight for the summit. They generally reach the "Balcony" at the base of the Southeast Ridge around sunrise, then continue along the ridge to the South Summit. From there, they negotiate a traverse to the Hillary Step, a 40-foot-high wall of rock and ice, which, when surmounted, puts them within an hour of the summit. Hopefully,

the climbers will return to Camp IV before dark, after 18 hours of climbing.

Camp IV was Camp VI in the early 1950s, and Camp VII then was placed on the Balcony, at 27,600 feet. Only a few believed that climbers could reach the summit and return to the South Col in a day. Though physically just as difficult, the summit push may be psychologically easier now. Climbers seem more willing to climb longer in exposed situations.

"Camp IV is needed, but it's basically a rest and rehydration stop," Ed noted. "You get there tired, make camp, spend time and energy making a meal, and after not getting any sleep you repeat the process in the morning."

ACCLIMATIZING DOES NOT MEAN ADJUSTING TO CLIMATE

Why all the moving up and down before the climb? The Sherpas and team are leapfrogging supplies from camp to camp, but they are also acclimatizing. Moving too high too fast can strain this process and lead to high-altitude illnesses.

Acclimatization is time-consuming. Most experienced Himalayan mountaineers recommend ascending no more than 2,000 feet a day, in order to give the body time to adjust to lower pressure and oxygen levels.

It's remarkable that humans can adjust to altitude to the extent they do. Without supplemental oxygen, a person used to living at sea level would collapse within a half hour and die soon afterward if suddenly taken to 20,000 feet. At the summit of Mount Everest—where the available oxygen is a third that at sea level—the same person would lose consciousness almost immediately and die within minutes.

The 3,000 vertical feet from Camp IV to the summit is supremely difficult. At extreme altitudes, physical performance decreases at an accelerating rate. Even though Everest is only 778 feet higher than K2—representing a difference in barometric

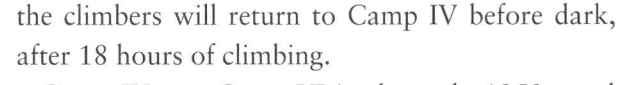

1996: **Not all of home's comforts—but many of them— surround *Everest* team members in their Base Camp dining tent.**

pressure of only 3 percent—there is a disproportionately much greater drop in the body's ability to obtain and utilize oxygen.

Everest is in a class by itself. Houston stressed that "the Everest summiter must climb the last thousands of feet relying on courage, determination, and drive, rather than on more acclimatization."

Indeed, after weeks above 20,000 feet, additional gains in terms of acclimatization are marginal. In Operation Everest, Houston found that humans deteriorate above this height even in the comfortable conditions of a decompression chamber. Dr. Peter Hackett, executive director of

> 66
> You don't just deal with adversity. You use it to **propel yourself forward.**
> ~ERIK WEIHENMAYER,
> IN *MOUNTAIN HEROES: PORTRAITS OF ADVENTURE*
> 99

the Institute for Altitude Medicine and an expert in high-altitude physiology, describes the slow degeneration that the team faces as "a slow death by starvation, dehydration, suffocation, and exposure."

Although they need to climb high for acclimatization, the team must limit their stay there. Much of the recent success on Everest has depended upon climbers fine-tuning this balance: acclimatizing just enough to summit before they are too debilitated to do so.

Individuals respond differently to altitude, but this is difficult to predict. Those whose bodies naturally cry out for more oxygen as they ascend actually acclimatize better

Climbers use fixed ropes to ascend the craggy ice of the Khumbu Icefall and pass below hanging seracs.

Sherpas navigate the vast expanse of the glacier-filled Western Cwm between Camps I and II.

than those whose bodies don't react as much to the decreased oxygen.

"We know little about why this is so," Houston once said, "but the major factors determining one's response to high altitude are the speed of ascent, the altitude reached, one's health at the time, and genetic or other influences.

"The fact is, we don't know how best to acclimatize," Houston continued with characteristic candor. "On the one hand, thousands of mountaineers have used the time-honored method of climbing slowly upward and descending to sleep—the siege tactic known as 'climb high, sleep low.'"

"Alpine style" is the other method, in which climbers live at Base Camp and scramble up nearby peaks, going a little higher each day, getting tough and acclimatized. When the weather and individual conditions match, they go for the summit in one shot. "Dozens of people have summited both Everest and K2 from Base Camp in this style, too," Houston added, "but some have died. It may be a riskier technique."

Whether climbers suffer brain damage from the hypoxia of a prolonged stay at altitude is hotly debated. Some have, the physiologists note, but usually these victims also experienced severe altitude illness, hypothermia, exhaustion, or trauma.

The team was fully aware of Houston's straightforward advice on acclimatizing: Take time to go high, don't overexert or overeat, drink extra water, and listen to your body.

And, as Jamling reminded them, listen to Miyolangsangma, the Maiden of the Wind.

CHAPTER FOUR

THE MOUNTAIN THAT ROSE FROM THE SEA

Climbers first viewed the Khumbu Icefall from the Nepal side in 1950, the year that Dr. Charles Houston joined the first group of foreigners to visit Khumbu. The group's journals, he said, consisted largely of superlatives expressing Khumbu's beauty and grandeur. But their glimpse of the Icefall itself was sobering. "For a long time we looked at the terrible icefall coming out of the Western Cwm, and decided that the approach would be very dangerous and difficult, perhaps impossible."

This maze of crevasses, seracs, and ice blocks the size of apartment buildings has claimed more lives than any other part of the mountain. Avalanches routinely thunder down from the Lhotse wall and Everest's Southwest Face, and wash over the glacier as they did in 2014 and 2015; chunks of ice weighing hundreds of tons shift and tumble without warning; seemingly bottomless crevasses open and close, albeit more slowly. Looking up at the Khumbu Icefall from Base Camp, one feels one is about to be deluged by a tidal wave of gigantic ice cubes.

The 1963 American Everest expedition, sponsored in part by the National Geographic Society, experienced the first death of a foreign climber on the

1996: **Fixed ropes and steel-toothed crampons enable a climber to walk up the Icefall's ice walls.**

Nepal side of Everest. Dr. Gil Roberts was leading the second rope through the Icefall, ten yards behind the climbers ahead, when a 30-foot freestanding wall of ice fell over and entombed his good friend Jake Breitenbach. Gil was partly buried, but freed himself and began digging out others.

With great emotion, Gil had to cut the rope that led to Jake, hopelessly buried beneath the serac. Then, as he helped the injured survivors descend through the Icefall, he heard a cry that sounded nearly human. It was a gorak, the bird believed to be the auspicious bearer of human souls, flying up from a crevice in the ice next to them.

Jake's body emerged from the Khumbu Glacier in 1970, and a fellow team member, Barry Bishop, took him for burial on the ridge beyond Tengboche.

Bishop had summited with the '63 expedition, and later served for many years on the National Geographic Society's Committee for Research and Exploration. He and his son Brent were the first American father and son to both summit Everest. In 1994 Bishop died in a car accident en route to receive an award from the American Himalayan Foundation honoring this achievement. At Tengboche, some of Bishop's ashes are now buried alongside Jake Breitenbach.

A SCARY KIND OF PLACE

The team would need the last three weeks of April to establish and stock the upper camps. But first they would need to get through the Icefall.

Customarily, the route through the Icefall is found and maintained by a single team, which is paid for this service by the other teams. In early spring before most expeditions had arrived at Base Camp, an international party led by Scottish climber Mal Duff explored the Icefall for the safest and most

> " It was titillating to brush up against the enigma of mortality, to steal a glimpse across its forbidden frontier. **Climbing was a magnificent activity,** I firmly believed, not in spite of the inherent perils, but precisely **because of them.**
>
> ~JON KRAKAUER,
> *INTO THIN AIR*
> "

direct route through it. They were followed by "rope teams" carrying ladders, 6,000 feet of rope, and plenty of hardware: 100 ice screws and 100 pickets (one-meter-long aluminum stakes), used to anchor the fixed ropes and the ladders over the crevasses. The danger from falling is greatly reduced by the use of fixed ropes, which are secured along exposed sections of the route for the duration of the season. Climbers have an ascending device, or carabiner, connected to their harness, and they clip this to the rope; they slide it up the rope as they climb, and the carabiner stops them if they fall.

More than 60 eight-foot aluminum ladder sections may be used in the Icefall. For a horizontal bridge, up to four sections are bolted together or lashed with plastic rope. Over the middle of the crevasse, many climbers lower to a crawl because of the unnerving bounce.

"A ladder like that is a little *wow*," Araceli recounted excitedly. "I look down, and then at my small rope—if I fall someone will catch me and take me out, I hope." Before her first Everest attempt last year, Araceli climbed some daunting vertical routes in Yosemite. By comparison, the Icefall was a snap, technically, but it gave her pause. "There's a place where sometimes you see your friends over there and get near them, on the same level, and then you go down again," she added. "It's a labyrinth of shifting turquoise ice. This is the challenging and fun part of the climb, but you must be there at not the wrong time."

Ed recalled a precarious stretch he encountered in '94. "To get up one ice headwall we used nine ladders tied end-to-end, with guylines leading off to

Porters carry ladders through the Icefall, for climbers to use later to cross deep crevasses.

the sides like trapeze wires. That was a crazy ride—it curved over backward near the top, and swayed horribly." The lower side of the crevasse dropped daily, and each morning Ed and his team found the topmost ladder another five feet below the upper lip. Each day a Sherpa would strap extra ladder sections to his back, crawl up the tottering construction, and lash them to the top end.

Once the Icefall ladders are fixed, they require daily maintenance to accommodate movement, especially later in the season. Screws melt out, the glacier moves, crevasses widen, and sometimes whole sections of the glacier collapse and take out the route. That is exactly what happened on April 18, 2014, when a major avalanche on the Icefall cost 16 climbing Sherpas their lives.

"Climbing through the Icefall is like trying to cross a busy interstate at night dressed in black clothes," wrote Jim Litch, a climber and a doctor at the Himalayan Rescue Association's Pheriche clinic. "The difference is that instead of doing it once, climbers make the trip over and over to the point that it becomes an acceptable risk."

On April 8, when Ed first climbed through it, he remarked that it was in the best shape and location he had ever seen it, due partly to the heavy winter and spring snowfall. No matter the conditions, climbers should travel it only in the early morning, when the ice bridges and seracs are more solidly frozen.

As summit day approached, the Sherpas climbed empty from Camp II to Camp III on the Lhotse Face, picked up loads and carried them to the South Col, then returned to Camp II the same evening.

Like the climbers, the Sherpas enjoy the challenge and competition, and many are as strong as the best climbers. "People who climb Everest boast of their success, but few of them mention that 95 percent of the work—the grunt work—was done by Sherpas," Ed commented. "I've noticed that the climbers and clients who talk most about reaching the summit tend to be those who avoid the day-to-day work needed to get them there. They're often the ones who get in trouble, too."

Ed doesn't ask the Sherpas to do anything he wouldn't. He works to create a rapport, cross-checks plans with them, and lets them know that he's not simply ordering them around. "I know I'll see them again next year, and I want to maintain a good working relationship—and to continue having a good time."

David and Robert created opportunities to film whenever they could. They set up the bulky camera in the Icefall, though they were unnerved by the conflicting demands of both moving quickly through the treacherous landscape and waiting for the proper light. They got

> **"**
> We have entered an era where it is **every man for himself,** particularly above 8,000 meters . . . Concern about the welfare of your companions seems to fade as the air gets thinner.
> ~SIR EDMUND HILLARY,
> *VOICES FROM THE SUMMIT*
> **"**

In 1953, Sherpas crossed log bridges wearing crampons—a task that wasn't meant for the faint of heart.

the shots they needed, despite one mishap. "Quick, a cloud is coming, we need to use this light!" David said to Robert during one precarious camera setup. "I tried to concentrate, but somehow turned the loading dial the wrong way," Robert recalled. "The camera ran up to speed, but the registration pins weren't positioned properly and they perforated new holes in the film. The camera jammed, making a real mess of the film. It was like celluloid confetti."

Only a few days earlier at Base Camp, the film crew had been shooting a time-lapse shot of golden clouds flowing past a silhouetted peak. The camera made an unusual noise, then began to smoke. Brad immediately thought of its magnesium construction: The camera itself could ignite. Acting quickly, he removed the lens, and a ring of electrical smoke blew out at him from inside the body of the camera. He traced the smoke to a faulty, inexpensive chip, a component they had been assured was bombproof. Fortunately, Brad Ohlund had brought a replacement with him, and the camera was running again in several hours.

The following day, several pairs of the team's crampons were stolen from the base of the icefall, where the climbers routinely left them while walking about on the rubble at Base Camp. David called a meeting of the team leaders to alert them, to request their return should they turn up, and to discuss the meaning of the theft in the context of the long tradition of mountaineering etiquette. At camp later,

Making history as part of the first American Everest expedition, Barry Bishop glories at the summit in 1963.

he told Steve Judson that he felt the incident was a bad omen.

RESCUE

The Icefall crevasses are so deep that when Sherpas look into their blue-black depths they often joke that they're "looking into America." Falling into one is referred to as "getting a visa to the U.S."

On April 8, a radio call announced that there had been an accident in the Western Cwm. An unroped Sherpa on Rob Hall's team had fallen through a snow bridge and into a hidden crevasse between Camp I and Camp II. Miraculously, he had landed on a peninsular ledge surrounded by darkness and depth. The Sherpa was pulled out by his teammates and was stranded at Camp I for two days with a suspected broken femur. The complicated evacuation involved 35 people, including six Everest team Sherpas, and took most of a day. From Base Camp the Sherpa was airlifted to Kathmandu. He was one of five sent by Rob Hall to establish Camp II before Hall had arrived at Base Camp and before Hall's Base Camp puja had been conducted. Some Sherpas connected the accident to this breach of tradition.

About two weeks later, Audrey reported that lights could be seen bobbing through the Icefall. Nawang Dorje, a Sherpa on Scott Fischer's team, had become sick and was assisted down by fellow team members on April 24. His symptoms of rales, caused by fluid in the lungs, resembled those of severe pulmonary edema, but when his condition didn't improve, doctors suspected it was complicated by other factors. Nawang remained in critical condition at the Pheriche clinic, at 14,000 feet, until he was evacuated to Kathmandu by helicopter when the weather finally cleared enough to fly on April 26.

Audrey also reported that a member of Mal Duff's party had experienced a suspected heart attack on April 20 while climbing, and that he had

(Continued on page 114)

1996: Sumiyo Tsuzuki navigates an aluminum ladder bridging a crevasse in the Khumbu Icefall.

The Icefall can be treacherous, especially for inexperienced climbers.

been evacuated to Kathmandu. Ten days later, a Danish climber on Mal Duff's team was injured while descending from Camp II and suffered broken ribs. David and Robert were nearby and found that the man could walk, albeit slowly and with difficulty. Robert and Thilen Sherpa elected to help him through the Icefall, where he was met by team members.

The team feared the likelihood of more accidents below Camp I. Many of the Taiwanese staggering through the Icefall didn't appear to belong on Everest: Some didn't know how to tie their crampons

on and had difficulty walking in them correctly. The South Africans, too, were having problems. During the trek in, their three most experienced climbers resigned over concerns about safety, and described the expedition leader Ian Woodall as extremely unprofessional. For the remainder of the season, the South African team did not share the spirit of cooperation that is nearly always found in the mountains.

Henry Todd, leading his own group, was concerned enough to give ice-climbing instructions to South African Deshun Deysel, who had never been on snow and ice before. It turned out that Ian Woodall had never confirmed her permit as an expedition member.

David detected a certain look shared by the inexperienced clients: wearing the right gear, but

(previous spread) Everest as seen from Kala Pattar: The sun lights up the mountain's peak like a beacon, leaving the Khumbu Icefall in shadow.

out of place and awkward in it. He made a point of taking time to speak with the ones he met, urging them to be extremely careful and reminding them of the more dangerous parts of the climb. Guides for the commercial groups, aware of many of their clients' inexperience, suggested establishing a rule about turnaround time. After some discussion it was agreed that on summit day, if clients had not summited by 2:00 p.m., they would have to return to the South Col. No guide would want to gather clients straggling back to Camp IV in the dark.

On April 30, the team returned to Base Camp. Camps II and III were established. Camp IV on the South Col had been stocked with oxygen, food, and other supplies. They were as acclimatized as they would get, and now needed as much as five days to rest and to regain some of the weight they had lost higher on the mountain.

One evening, a raucous party was held at Rob Hall's dining tent. Some climbers privately questioned why someone would have a party before the summit attempt. Others could understand the need to let off some steam; the combined tension of weather, logistics, crowding, and the dangerous mission of climbing the mountain had been building. For Hall, the stakes may have been raised: Neither he nor any of his party had reached the summit the

> 66
>
> There is, in man, **an essential paradox.** On the one hand he seeks all the ways and means to make his life more comfortable, safe, and certain; but, on the other, he knows intuitively that only by taking risks and facing up to uncertainty is he going to **stretch himself, go beyond himself.**
>
> ~DOUG SCOTT,
>
> *VOICES FROM THE*
>
> *SUMMIT*
>
> 99

year before, and this year he had two additional clients.

At dinner the team seemed relaxed. Each had reached Camp III and had returned safely. "The interesting part for me is the *missing* mountain—what erosion took away," Roger commented one evening with playful irony. "Everyone here seems awestruck by the stuff that was left behind."

"THIS ENTIRE RANGE LAY BENEATH THE OCEAN"

Even the summit of Everest contains rocks that were formed of sediments from an ancient sea—or seas. The 450-million-year-old marine limestone deposits on Everest may have been to the tops of mountain ranges and back to the sea more than once, and ten million years hence the eroded remnants of Everest may again be on the bottom of the Indian Ocean. "In as soon as several thousand years from now—a mere geological instant—it is likely that Everest will cease to be the world's tallest mountain," Roger explained in an impromptu lecture that followed dinner one evening. "At some point, its top will succumb to gravity and simply fall down the slope in a big landslide."

Because they are so dynamic, the Himalaya are one of the earth's great laboratories for the study of mountain building and erosion. In Khumbu,

---

FLASH FORWARD **MICHAEL GROOM**

Australian Michael Groom was 40 years old when he climbed Makalu in 1999, completing his goal to climb the world's five highest peaks. He climbed all five without bottled oxygen and climbed all but Kangchenjunga without the front third of his feet, which he lost to frostbite in 1987. He serves as a motivational speaker and has written a book about his climbing adventures and philosophy called *Sheer Will*. He plans to return to the Himalaya to attempt the Southwest Ridge of Ama Dablam.

THE HIGHEST FAULT IN THE WORLD

Several fault types played an important role in the evolution of the Himalaya: The two most significant are thrust faults and normal faults. Thrust faults mark the zones along which sheets of continental crust are shoved over other sheets.

If you've ever watched a snowplow at work, you've seen sheets of crusted snow piled up in front of the snowplow's blade. In much the same way, sheets of rock are piled up to form the thickened crust of a mountain range.

Normal faults develop in a different way: They thin rather than thicken the crust. Lay a deck of cards on a table and spread them out with your hand. This causes each card to slip past adjacent cards the same way that normal faults move, resulting in a wider but thinner stack of cards. Normal faults are usually found in regions of crustal thinning, like the East African Rift, rather than in mountainous regions. Their existence in the Himalaya implies that the range did not grow higher and thicken continuously throughout its history, but experienced intermittent episodes of thinning and collapse. These probably occurred when the crust of the range became too hot and weak to support its own weight.

One of the most spectacular of the Himalayan normal faults is the Chomolungma detachment. It occurs near the summit of Everest, cropping out on the North Face at an elevation of 27,953 feet, where Japanese geologist Minoru Sawada studied it in 1998. Before this discovery, geologists had predicted the position of the fault based on studies in the Rongbuk Valley to the north of the massif. There the detachment is tilted very shallowly northward, separating Ordovician limestones above (between 458 and 485 million years old) from older metamorphic rocks below. One of the rock units just below the fault is a band of yellow marble deposited as a limestone in the Cambrian period,

Everest's peak is continually shifting upward.

then metamorphosed to marble much later during the Miocene epoch. Based on aerial photographs and field observations, the fault could be traced southward toward the mountain. From near the summit of Everest, climbers had collected rocks similar to the Ordovician limestones in the Rongbuk Valley. This, with other evidence, led geologists to speculate that the yellow marble in the Rongbuk Valley is the same rock as the famous Yellow Band, one of the most conspicuous landmarks for climbers on Everest. If so, that would put the Chomolungma detachment somewhere between the Yellow Band and the summit, perhaps at the top of the Yellow Band.

To help test this hypothesis, the 1996 *Everest* film team collected rock samples within and just above the Yellow Band. Samples brought back from other expeditions require the fault to be below the Hillary Step, but its exact position remained a matter of speculation until Minoru Sawada's discovery in 1998. The Chomolungma detachment is almost certainly the highest major fault in the world.

A hiker lights up the Khumbu Glacier, where layers of rock and sediment hold stories about climate change.

the geology is immediately apparent, particularly above the tree line where there is little vegetation to conceal the cliffs and rocks.

Standing near Base Camp, Roger seemed to say, *Now it all makes sense*, as he turned and surveyed the stony mountainscape. Jamling saw him bend over to pick up yet another wayside rock.

"Put that down," Jamling gibed. "We may be carrying some of your scientific devices to the South Col for you, but don't ask us to start carrying *rocks!*"

Roger Bilham has helped pioneer the use of GPS receivers to measure the movement of the surface of the Earth. Teams of students from the University of Colorado and Caltech, led by Jean-Philippe Avouac along with local scientists from Nepal, have now obtained considerable information about the

processes of tectonic collision in the Nepal Himalaya. With the use of signals from GPS satellites, either recorded continuously or for several days and repeated at yearly or greater intervals, the relative positions of these points throughout the mountains have been measured to an accuracy of one to three millimeters. A permanently fixed unit was installed when the expedition passed through Namche Bazar, but GPS measurements have now been made at hundreds of points throughout the Himalaya.

The observations of vertical and horizontal motion are then combined with information about microseismicity and geological structure. "By mapping all of this, we can infer the style and rate of deformation at depth and in turn gain insight into the potential of future earthquakes," Roger explained.

Robert and David accompanied Roger up Kala Pattar, or "Black Rock," a relatively small peak overlooking Base Camp. Kala Pattar rocks are covered with a dark layer of "desert varnish" caused by thousands of years of solar radiation; when broken open, the rock is actually a light-colored granite. There, Roger activated one of the solar-powered GPS receivers, to measure and calculate the distances to Lukla, Pheriche, Dingboche, and Tengboche, where GPS readings were taken during the expedition. The climbers would take a sixth reading on Everest's South Col, an unwieldy but valuable location.

Khumbu's valleys are covered with loose glacial moraine and their sides are too steep for the receiver. The relatively flat South Col has excellent sky visibility and is located on bedrock that is free of snow. "As long as someone else will haul the device up there, I'm delighted," Roger said.

The eight GPS navigational satellites broadcast on the same frequency, but to a stationary receiver their frequencies appear to shift because they are moving relative to each other—like the changing sound of a high-speed train whistle when it passes an observer. The GPS receiver is programmed with satellite satellite location.

The GPS receiver is programmed with satellite location.
tions and contains a very precise clock, which allows the unit to distinguish between satellites and thereby calculate its location.

The GPS measurements showed that Namche Bazar is converging on Rongbuk monastery, directly north of Everest, at the rate of nearly a half inch per year. "Our measurements indicate that the Indian plate is sliding northward beneath Tibet along an inclined plane roughly ten miles below Namche," Roger explained. "Above that plane, rocks scraped off the Indian plate are caught in the squeeze between India and Tibet, and are thrust upward."

GREAT EARTHQUAKES ARE INEVITABLE

In the past three decades, GPS measurements have established that convergence between southern Tibet and northern India varies from a low of 12 millimeters a year (mm/yr) in the west to a high of 18 mm/yr in the center of the Himalayan arc, dropping to about 16 mm/yr in the east. Thus the Indian plate is descending beneath the Himalaya at around three-quarters of an inch per year. "Prithvi Narayan Shah, founder of modern Nepal in 1768, described

1996: Documenting the Icefall's drama, David Breashears trains his lens on Araceli as she navigates the vertical ice.

Nepal as "a gourd being squeezed between two hard rocks," Roger said. "He was expressing a political sentiment when he wrote this, but the analogy holds up just as well in the geophysical sense."

Because of the enormous forces of friction that must be overcome for India to slide northward beneath the Himalaya, the zone of contact between the Himalaya and India holds fast for hundreds of years until sufficient force has built up to overcome this friction. Where there are no great earthquakes, the plates aren't slipping, but rather are squeezing the Himalaya, "like the winding of a terrific spring," Roger explained. "The resulting buildup of elastic energy must eventually be released in the form of a catastrophic quake. In mere moments, parts of the Himalaya south of us may leap five meters—and possibly more than ten meters—toward the plains of India." So how much time must elapse before this convergent stress overcomes friction at the base of the Himalaya?

A clue can be found in the surface ruptures of historical earthquakes. We know that great earthquakes start in the north beneath the high peaks and rupture 58 miles southward, moving the mountains and villages of Nepal dozens of feet southward, ending roughly 30 seconds later in a visible earthquake scarp, a 10- to 30-foot-high wall of elevated soil and rock flung southward over forests and fields, offsetting roads and fracturing pipes, and creating instant

(Continued on page 122)

when combined with the three-quarter-inch-per-year convergence observed from GPS measurements, means that the 1934 rupture allowed eastern Nepal to slip almost 42 feet southward over the Indian plate. On June 6, 1515, a huge earthquake ruptured through the Himalaya. Monasteries in the Thakola region were destroyed, as was the then-new Moghul capital of Agra to the south. The earthquake heaved a wall of soil 20 feet high over the fields and forests of medieval India. At three-quarters of an inch per year, this kind of monumental quake (M 8.9) can't occur more frequently than once in 1,000 years. If the pattern repeats, then a similar rupture won't happen for another five centuries.

But what about the remainder of the Himalayan arc? Some of the most recent severe Himalayan

waterfalls, as seen in Kashmir in 2005. The same thing happened in Nepal in 1934, when a magnitude (M) 8.4 earthquake caused catastrophic damage in eastern Nepal and in villages throughout the Ganges plain to the south. No one noticed the surface rupture in 1934 because it occurred far from the main road to Kathmandu. The rupture was discovered in 2012 by a Nepali-French team of geologists led by Paul Tapponnier, and excavations showed not only evidence for at least 15 feet of slip in 1934, but also for a historically known earthquake in 1255, which destroyed Kathmandu and killed the reigning monarch. The 679 years between these two earthquakes,

1996: Clouds ominously begin to run up the Western Cwm, dubbed the "Valley of Silence" by climbers in 1952.

earthquakes, in 1950 (M 8.6 in Assam) and 2005 (M 7.6 in Kashmir), occurred at the extreme ends of the arc. A small segment northwest of Delhi slipped in 1905 (M 7.8 in Kangra), with some other modest events in 1803 and 1833. An earthquake in 2015 (M 7.9 near Kathmandu) occurred at the middle of the arc, devastating Nepal's capital and villages throughout the region.

EARTHQUAKE STUDIES
Because of the wedgelike shape of the Himalaya and the Ganges sediments—15 miles thick in the north, tapering to nothing south of the Ganges plain—the seismic waves of energy emanating from the quake nucleus will be focused southward and become trapped within the gradually narrowing bands of Himalayan sediment in southern Nepal and northern India. As a result, the dense populations of these areas could experience a more severe jolt than those living closer to the nucleus of the quake itself.

During the Great Bihar Earthquake of 1934, this focusing effect increased ground-shaking accelerations by more than a factor of two compared to points on solid rock south of the Ganges plains. Tens of thousands died. If that earthquake were to recur today, the death and destruction would likely be much greater, partly because of the fact that Kathmandu's population has doubled in the past several decades and partly because of the surge in the number of buildings that are taller and poorly constructed.

A major earthquake in 2015 confirmed seismologists' fears and cost thousands of Kathmandu residents their lives.

Everest and surrounding mountains as seen from the International Space Station

> **There were many, many fine reasons not to go, but attempting to climb Mt. Everest is an intrinsically irrational act—a triumph of desire over sensibility.** Any person who would seriously consider it is almost by definition beyond the sway of reasoned argument.
>
> **~JON KRAKAUER, INTO THIN AIR**

"Unfortunately, public officials are reluctant to believe that the recurrence of nightmare earthquakes is inevitable," Roger says, "and damaging moderate earthquakes don't occur with sufficient frequency to remind people of the dangers of poor-quality construction. So, wherever I go in the Himalaya, I publicize earthquakes, especially among urban planners."

ANTICIPATION
Like David and Ed, other expedition leaders were concerned by the number of teams on the mountain and the potential for a jam. To avert the costly and potentially dangerous consequences of unanticipated delays, Scott Fischer and Rob Hall conferred on the timing of their teams' summit attempts. Before even reaching Base Camp, Hall had wanted to try for the summit on May 10. In previous years he had gone for the top on this day, and he had the feeling it was lucky: Nearly all his clients had reached the summit in 1994, though no clients had summited in '95.

Initially, Fischer wanted to try on May 9. But when he discussed with Hall the shortage of time and the manpower needed to fix ropes high on the mountain, they decided to combine their experienced staffs. They chose May 10 as summit day for both teams, then notified the other expedition leaders, suggesting they plan around their date. Later parties, they explained, would benefit by the fixed ropes Fischer's and Hall's teams would leave behind on the tricky Hillary Step and the summit ridge.

David, Ed, and Robert had climbed Everest without fixed ropes above the South Col, and they knew that Jamling, Araceli, and Sumiyo could do so as well. They chose May 9, a day ahead of the two large groups. For the purposes of the film and for safety, David wanted the team to be relatively alone on summit day.

FROM BASE CAMP TO THE WESTERN CWM

On May 5, the team lit incense at the lhap-so and departed Base Camp for Camp II. "A part of me is excited and curious about what will happen," Araceli said, "and another part of me is afraid. But this fear is what makes me respect the mountain."

David maintained a positive but cautious attitude. "We're right on schedule and if the weather holds, if we remain healthy, and if the camera doesn't malfunction, we should be able to get on top and get these images."

The climbers emerged from the Icefall at 19,800 feet just as the sun hit, and walked onto the massive glacial snowfield known as the Western Cwm (pronounced KOOM, a Welsh word that means "valley" or "cirque"). They deployed their umbrellas to block the powerful sunlight. The snow blanketing this low-angle valley acts like a giant solar oven, concentrating the sun that reflects off the walls of Nuptse, off the western buttress of Everest, and from the broad glacier valley that extends below them.

"When people think of Everest, they think of cold and wind. But some of the more uncomfortable

In recent years, dense lines of climbers traversing the Lhotse Face have caused anxiety about overcrowding.

conditions here are caused by excessive heat," David explained. "The ambient temperature in the Western Cwm can be well below freezing, yet you can't remove enough clothes to stay cool. We pray for a gust of wind, and when it comes our work capacity immediately rises."

Losing fluid through sweating—in addition to the large amount exhaled by heavy breathing—increases the risk of dehydration, which causes a wide range of symptoms and problems. "I'm trying to drink two to three liters of water a day, on rest days alone," Ed said. "When climbing, we should drink at least twice that, but at high altitudes we're often not thirsty. There's also the disincentive of having to get up in the middle of the night."

Camp II is set in the majestic, sculpted cirque of the upper end of the Western Cwm. The Southwest Face rises more than 7,000 vertical feet above camp and seems to disappear into the stratosphere. Though temperatures at Camp II were still dipping below zero at night, the days were warmer than when the team first arrived almost a month earlier. In the afternoons, water flowed and gurgled over the rocks and made rivulets in the snow.

On May 7 the team left Camp II, slowed only by their moderate pace and by the bergschrund, or crevasse, at the base of the Lhotse Face. Robert recalled that two weeks earlier Yasuko Namba, who was not entirely confident using an ice ax, had to be pulled up the 50 vertical feet of the bergschrund by a Sherpa.

> **"**
> Getting to the top is optional, **getting back down is mandatory.** A lot of people forget about that.
>
> ~ED VIESTURS,
> *NO SHORTCUTS*
> *TO THE TOP*
> **"**

At the ledge on top, Sumiyo met Namba, and the two nodded and bowed while they spoke politely. "They were clearly wishing each other the best of luck," Robert said, "but I could sense something of an air of competition between them."

The team climbed the steep Lhotse Face to Camp III, where tent sites had been carved out of the face itself. High winds continued to blast the Southeast Ridge far above them, and a mood of nervous tension prevailed. Their faces were swollen and sunburned, and they spoke little about the mountain.

Ed stirred a pot balanced on a small stove. "Well, we'll have some beef stroganoff for dinner, although Spam and Dijon mustard would be a more complete meal. Spam is high in protein, it comes out in convenient chunks, and you get 170 calories from only two ounces!" Araceli rolled her eyes.

Sumiyo turned the videotape camera on Ed, and he conveyed a message to Paula. The cassette would be taken to Base Camp by a Sherpa the next morning. "We're heading up to the South Col tomorrow," Ed said confidently. "Please don't worry about me."

"I'm worried, myself," Araceli interjected quietly off camera, "mostly about being cold."

Sumiyo finished the taping and turned to Araceli. "Which socks will you wear for the summit?" She was aware of Araceli's problem with slow circulation.

"Oh, I can't decide between the red ones and the pink ones," Araceli feigned. She had commented

FLASH FORWARD **BROUGHTON COBURN**

Coburn is a writer, lecturer, and college instructor who specializes in crafting narratives of the people and landscape of the Himalaya. Since 1996, he has written a young adult photobiography of Sir Edmund Hillary, *Triumph on Everest;* co-wrote Jamling Tenzing Norgay's autobiography, *Touching My Father's Soul;* and written *The Vast Unknown,* which explores the first American ascent of Everest, in 1963. He often speaks publicly, and some of his lectures vividly recount the events and the context of the 1996 season on Everest and the IMAX film expedition.

earlier that modern climbing gear may be lighter and warmer, but that the mountain hasn't changed. "Your equipment and your body must be ready, but summit day will be the most difficult because you are weak even when you start out. It will be the other climbers, the team, and the teamwork that will determine whether we reach the top."

Three days earlier, Sumiyo had cracked a rib from violent coughing. She had cracked another one three weeks before that, while establishing the high camps. Though this injury is painful, little can be done to treat it. "My cough hasn't stopped, but my ribs seem to be improving," she said optimistically. The rest of the team looked at her with sympathy and hope, knowing how much she wanted to try for the summit and to install Roger's GPS and weather stations. "You know, I didn't tell my father that I was coming here to climb Everest," she added, sensing their concern.

"Now she tells us," Ed said.

"We're strong, and the rest days were good," Jamling said optimistically. "But I miss my wife, and my daughter will be ten months old tomorrow. I'll have to try to concentrate on the climb."

As they had done on many nights, at Camp III David and Robert spent two hours cleaning and checking the IMAX camera and equipment. Robert worked long into the night loading film magazines with the bulky large-format film.

The team watched the upper part of the mountain. And listened. Fierce winds out of Tibet were still funneling over the South Col, threatening to drop into the Western Cwm. Robert called these gales, which sounded like freight trains, the "Lhasa-Kathmandu Express." Climbers caught in the middle of them describe the sound as varying between a deafening roar and an endless, nerve-rattling howl that flaps

Climbers often use fixed ropes up the Lhotse Face.

tents so violently that it's nearly impossible to talk. Sleep is difficult.

While establishing Camp III several days earlier, David saw a tent blow past him at 60 mph; on a previous expedition he had seen all the dining tents at Camp II get blasted away. "Your tent will be quiet for 15 seconds, then is suddenly barraged for minutes at a time," he grimaced.

The wind saps what small amount of warmth a hypoxic person is able to generate; Ed knew that summiting, particularly without bottled oxygen, would require a relatively calm day. Each year in May, there is a period of a few days when the high winds and unpredictable weather subside, presenting a window of clear and relatively calm weather. "That's the time to go for it," Ed attested, like a fisherman imparting a secret stratagem. "But if it turns bad, you have to be willing to retreat and wait."

For the climbers, weather is a gamble: It can start out fine and suddenly turn worse on climbs to the higher camps. And a bad day on Everest can be deadly. "There have been days in the past few weeks when we could have climbed Everest as mountaineers," David said, "but not as a film team. I have to be able to hold the camera steady and change the film bare-handed."

Robert had filmed in extreme conditions before, on a British expedition to the unclimbed Northeast Ridge. "The severe wind and weather kept us off the route for nearly two months, and during the summit push I had to turn back when my fingers froze while filming."

30 CLIMBERS, HEADING UP

That evening, the team looked down into the Western Cwm from Camp III and watched a stream of more than 30 people heading to Camp II. The group included two Taiwanese climbers and some Sherpas and guides, but most were clients of Scott Fischer and Rob Hall. Every one of them would be heading up to Camp III the following day.

Ed and David didn't need to speak. "We knew right then," Ed recalls, "that we did not want to summit on May 9." The descent from Everest's upper slopes is the single most dangerous part of the climb. The team would need to pass these climbers on their way down from the summit, and would have to unclip their carabiners from the fixed line and then reclip, many times, to get around people with unknown mountaineering skills. Would the clients step on the

Helicopters have to maneuver the thin air in the upper Khumbu, which makes quick air rescues a mighty challenge.

EVEREST WITHOUT OXYGEN

The debate over the use of supplemental oxygen in extreme-altitude climbing began during the first attempts on Everest in the 1920s and has continued ever since. "When I think of mountaineering with four cylinders of oxygen on one's back and a mask over one's face—well, it loses its charm," George Mallory wrote. But his colleague J. P. Farrar, an influential member of the British Alpine Club, countered: "Strictly speaking, I do not think that oxygen is any more of an artificial aid than food."

That mountaineers can climb "oxygenless" in the Death Zone highlights a coincidence of human and planetary evolution: The highest point on Earth is also the highest point at which the human body can function without supplementary oxygen. If it were very much higher, the summit would likely be unreachable without supplemental oxygen.

At that altitude, simply surviving—not to mention climbing upward—is no easy task. "When you run out of bottled O's at those altitudes, you might as well be underwater," observed climbing guide Pete Athans. "You retreat within yourself. You slow down."

Climbers are chronically hypoxic, and they report that the skin of other climbers has a bluish cast to it. "Your body turns into a machine to process whatever oxygen molecules it can find in the thin air," David Breashears noted. Reinhold Messner said that on his first oxygen-free ascent of Everest, with Peter Habeler in 1978, he felt he had become "nothing more than a single, narrow, gasping lung, floating over the mists and the summits."

Although our energy for metabolism comes from food, oxygen is the catalyst for the metabolic process, and its presence determines whether or not we can exert effort. "It's eerie," Ed Viesturs said. "If you turn someone's oxygen off, they stop moving. With oxygen you function better, think more clearly, stay warmer, and are able to climb steadily without pausing every step to suck in six or eight gasping breaths."

If oxygen is so precious, why do climbers climb without it?

Ed Viesturs climbed all fourteen 8,000ers without "O's."

"When I first attempt a Himalayan peak," Ed explained, "I climb without bottled oxygen, even if it keeps me from reaching the summit. My personal goal is to see how I can perform, to experience the mountain as it is without reducing it to my level. For me, how I reach the top is more important than whether I do."

At the summit, supplementary oxygen effectively "lowers" one by only 2,000 to 4,000 feet, making a small and yet significant difference to oxygen-starved climbers.

"Once climbers are on oxygen," Ed continued, "they become stronger. But it's a bit of a crutch. Without it, I don't have a mechanical apparatus that can fail on me and thereby endanger me.

"Most important, I'm aware of the tricks that altitude and hypoxia can play on you. While climbing, I test myself, asking myself whether I'm aware of the conditions, of my actions, and of what is around me. Exhaustion and hypoxia can cause one to 'lose it' mentally, and I never allow myself to fall into this state.

"When I'm guiding, however, I always use oxygen. You're there for the clients, and oxygen does enable you to function better, both physically and mentally."

Those settling in at Camp II turn lights on as night makes it harder to see over the vast expanse of the Western Cwm.

rope and cut it with their crampons? Dislodge some ice or rock? "Their presence gave me a sense of being squeezed," David said.

Ed and David agreed that the team should descend to Camp II. They would wait for the others to "climb through." Besides, the moderate break in weather did not appear to be the traditional early to mid-May window of clearing, and waiting might also result in more favorable weather conditions.

While they were on their way down on May 8, the other groups ascended past them. David said he felt uneasy, as if he were bailing out on the mountain and his friends on other teams. Just above Camp II, Robert passed Rob Hall near the bergschrund at the bottom of the Lhotse Face. Despite the fact that the team was being extremely careful, Hall was concerned about falling ice or rocks that David and

Bangladeshi climber Wasfia Nazreen clips onto a fixed rope on the Lhotse Face, where a mistake can spell disaster.

the team might dislodge onto his group. On the other hand, Robert felt that Hall might benefit by focusing his concern on the clients. Some of them were already on oxygen, though most climbers begin using it only above Camp III.

"The ankles of some were wobbling," Robert said. Not a positive sign. Shortly afterward, a rock that was likely set loose by an ascending climber whizzed by within a foot or two of Robert's head. Araceli expressed the wisdom and experience of a true mountaineer. "Yes, when you pass people on the way down, you think maybe we didn't make the right decision—maybe tomorrow the weather will improve. But turning back is never a bad decision. It gives you the chance to try again."

Another Catalan woman was attempting Everest from the north side, but Araceli said she felt no competition to be the first Spanish woman on Everest. "If you race when you are in the mountains, you lose the safe part of your mind," she said without hesitation.

131

A DEATH ON THE MOUNTAIN

Early in the morning of May 8, Chen Yu-Nan, a 36-year-old steelworker from Taipei, left his tent at Camp III on the steep Lhotse Face, possibly to relieve himself. He wasn't wearing crampons, and slipped 60 feet down the face and into a 15-foot crevasse. A Sherpa pulled him out.

Chen told "Makalu" Gau Ming-Ho, the leader of the Taiwanese team, that he would remain at Camp III, and assured him he would be all right. Believing his team member's condition to be fine, Gau departed for Camp IV alongside the Hall and Fischer teams.

Later in the day, the *Everest* team Sherpas returned to Camp III from the South Col. They found Chen in some distress, apparently suffering from internal injuries. They began to lead him down the fixed ropes. He was losing strength, but walking.

At 3 p.m., the Sherpas radioed Camp II that his condition had deteriorated.

A half hour later they called again. Chen had collapsed about two-thirds of the way down the Lhotse Face, and they now believed him to be dead. They left his body attached to the rope and descended to Camp II.

Lying on the slope, Chen was visible from Camp II. David insisted that they check on his condition— there was a chance he might be unconscious. The weather had turned rough, but David, Robert, and Ed packed quickly and departed. When they reached the Taiwanese climber, they could barely see through the blowing snow. Chen was dead.

At least they could evacuate his body. The Sherpas would not use the fixed rope as long as a body was attached to it, although monks remind lay Sherpas that it can actually be propitious to see dead bodies, especially in dreams or when traveling. Nonetheless, many of the Sherpa are averse to seeing or handling them, which can bring defilement, and thereby bad fortune, especially if there is a "karmic link" to the deceased.

By 2012, bottlenecking on the way to Camp III had become even more pronounced than it was in 1996.

A rescue helicopter makes the harrowing flight out of Base Camp during the 2012 National Geographic expedition.

David, Robert, and Ed lowered Chen to the foot of the Lhotse Face and over the bergschrund. After packing him in a sleeping bag, they dragged the dead climber back to Camp II and left him nearby in the ice. He could be carried down by his teammates later.

When Ed radioed Makalu Gau on the South Col to tell him that his climbing partner was dead, Makalu did not seem to take in the news. He was so utterly focused on getting himself to the summit that he answered vaguely, "Oh . . . thank you very much."

"I was upset by Makalu Gau's decision to leave Chen and continue climbing, because his death affected me," David said. "I had to go up and bring down a dead Taiwanese climber. I had to close his eyes and cover his face. I didn't like doing that; it was a senseless death."

It wasn't David's first experience with death on the mountain. In 1984, Dick Bass and David attempted Everest with the ill-fated Nepalese Clean-up Expedition. Team members Yogendra Thapa and Ang Dorjee fell from the Southeast Ridge to the South Col. Sherpas stuffed their frozen bodies into a tent, but eventually the tent came loose and fell another 4,000 feet to the Western Cwm. Climbing together again in 1985, David found parts of their frozen bodies, which had shattered when they hit the bottom. He collected what he could and dropped the body parts into a crevasse.

"On the north side in 1986," David said sadly, "a Sherpa named Dawa Nuru was swept away by an avalanche. Ang Phurba and I found him, and several Sherpas helped us get his body to Base Camp.

A lama was called, and he was cremated at the nunnery. When you see bodies, you don't have room for hysteria or emotions—it's a survival mechanism. But we do try to bring them down, to bring some closure for their relatives."

Jamling was troubled by the death of Chen, which occurred on the tenth anniversary of his father's death. At Camp II, he burned incense, prayed, and chanted. Those at Base Camp did the same at the lhap-so.

By the ninth of May, a Scandinavian, a Frenchman, two Spanish brothers, and Göran Kropp, the lone Swede, had made unsuccessful summit attempts via the South Col route. Three of them had reached the South Summit, at 28,710 feet, or just below it, but were forced back by deep snow and high winds. Also, a Yugoslav team had tried for the summit on May 9, but abandoned their attempt above the South Summit. They arrived on the South Col at 7 p.m., exhausted. Audrey reported that one member ran out of energy a few feet from the tents and had to be hauled inside.

Like the team members and many others, Charles Houston was humbled by the mountain's size and austerity. "Man does not conquer a mountain any more than a mountain conquers man," he had written in 1953. "For a few brief minutes, once in a million years, men have reached the summit of Everest and other high peaks. But how much more often have they been chased away, victims of bad luck, storm, or their own weakness. 'Surely the gods live here,' said Kipling's Kim, and he was speaking for many who have been awed by this magnificence."

Though this was Ed's eighth trip to Everest, he was approaching the mountain with similar humility, expressed in a practical way: "You don't assault Everest. You sneak up on it, and then get the hell outta there."

1996: Clipped into fixed ropes for safety, climbers string out on the lower Lhotse Face near Camp III. Upon reaching the sprawling Yellow Band—a distinctive geological layer, visible here—they will head left toward the Geneva Spur.

• CHAPTER FIVE •

TRAGEDY STRIKES

It was an hour past noon on May 10, yet Rob Hall's and Scott Fischer's teams were still high on Everest, striving toward the summit, knowing that descent in the dark was likely. Cold, exhausted, and hypoxic, the guides and climbers would also face the wind and rough weather that had been settling in on the mountain nearly every afternoon for the past month. By midafternoon, Base Camp had received radio calls from the summit. Audrey sat bundled at her laptop computer, and her

cold fingers tapped out the day's news for the satellite fax: "Today . . . Rob Hall, with two other guides and three of his clients (Jon Krakauer of *Outside* magazine, a Japanese woman, Yasuko Namba, and Doug Hansen) along with three Sherpas, and nine members of Scott Fischer's group . . . reached the summit . . . We understand Makalu Gau, leader of the tragic Taiwanese expedition, also made it up. However, all

the ascents were around 2 in the afternoon, which is very late in the day. We are now anxiously awaiting news that all of the climbers make it safely back to Col tonight."

Incredibly, 23 people had summited. But at Camp II the response to this news was guarded. "They are making the top in middle of the afternoon? *Whooof!*" Araceli said, expelling air in surprise and

1996: **Barely able to see amid rapidly worsening weather, the *Everest* team heads to Camp II.**

worry. Ed scanned the radio, but overheard only one conversation: Scott Fischer was telling his climbing sirdar to inform Rob Hall that three of Hall's clients had abandoned their attempt short of the summit, below the Hillary Step.

Ed, David, and Robert turned and looked from Camp II down the Western Cwm, in the direction of Base Camp. In the distance, they saw a large cloud bank welling up. At around 4 p.m. it began to roll toward them. At the same time, another cloud bank enveloped the upper mountain, several thousand feet above.

At 4:30 p.m., Paula was making potato soup in the team's Base Camp kitchen. Geodetic engineer Dave Mencin came over from Rob Hall's camp and informed her that he had just overheard a chilling radio conversation between Hall and his guide Andy Harris. Hall, who was still above the South Summit, was yelling to Harris that their client Doug Hansen had collapsed and needed oxygen. Hall said he would be staying there to help Hansen.

This was clearly a life-and-death situation. Paula dropped everything, and when she emerged from the cook tent, she looked up and saw thick, dark clouds moving extremely fast into Base Camp from down the valley.

"It was eerie; in two seasons at Base Camp, I'd never seen clouds like that," she said. "They were dark, purplish black."

Locally generated clouds tended to roll up the valley each afternoon, but these were more ominous. When Audrey stepped outside, she was so astonished by their appearance that she called Changba and the other Sherpas to take a look. They took time to examine them, then pressed their lips together tightly. No one spoke.

It began to snow. Paula ran to Rob's camp, but heard no further communication from Rob or others on the upper mountain. She radioed Ed and David at Camp II.

They were stunned. Rob Hall had decided to stay with client Doug Hansen near the dangerously high and exposed South Summit, knowing that he couldn't get him down alone. Hall and Hansen were undoubtedly exhausted; their oxygen may have run out; and now they were struggling through a pitch-dark whiteout, in a roaring, chilling wind.

"I tried to imagine what they were going through," Ed said. "A nightmare." High on the Southeast Ridge, the wind maintained a distant, menacing howl. David and Ed left the radio on.

CONFUSION ON THE COL

Some time after 8 p.m., Paula again radioed Ed and the team at Camp II. Information from Camp IV was sketchy, but Base Camp had heard that just a few of the 23 summiters and other climbers on the upper mountain had returned to their tents on the South Col. Only those who descended quickly from the summit or who had turned around before the top had arrived at camp. No one knew where the others were.

David and Ed knew what it was like to return to the South Col from the summit. "You're exhausted, and when you find your tent, you crawl into it and assume the climbers behind you made it into camp," Ed explained. "You don't want to get up and check on anything, or even walk around—you just want to pass out."

A short distance from camp, a tragedy was unfolding. Not far above the Col, high winds and snow had begun to buffet the returning climbers. Because of the danger of climbing down a steep section of

> " We had seen a whole mountain range, little by little, the lesser to the greater until, incredibly higher in the sky than **imagination had ventured to dream,** the top of Everest itself appeared.
>
> ~GEORGE MALLORY, IN *FEARLESS ON EVEREST: THE QUEST FOR SANDY IRVINE* "

Weather can deteriorate quickly on Everest, no matter how bright and promising the day might look.

rock-hard ice above the Col known as the "ice bulge" in the deteriorating conditions, one group of 11 climbers headed slightly east of the route they had ascended. By the time they reached the Col, darkness had fallen.

The Col is the size of several football fields and nearly as flat, resembling a vast, featureless plain. The raging storm limited visibility to a few feet, and when the climbers removed their dark-lensed ski goggles to see in the darkness, they had to squint into 60-mile-an-hour winds and driving snow. They were cold, hypoxic, tired, hungry, and dehydrated—all of which reduced circulation to their hands and feet, and dulled their minds.

At Base Camp, members from every group gathered at Rob Hall's camp. Many had radios in their hands and were attempting to communicate with the climbers still on the mountain. The batteries on Scott Fischer's radios had died, and no one could reach climbers on his team.

"Our heads were spinning with unanswered questions," Paula said. "Our worst fears and best-case scenarios swam together in our heads. I slept half an hour that night. Mattresses covered the floor of Rob's communication tent, where 15 people were curled up like sleeping dogs, dozing fitfully."

The tent was mostly silent except for some sporadic crying and praying. The Sherpas stayed up playing cards. All were desperate for information,

> **"**
> It was the **worst story idea** an editor could come up with, let alone assign to a real human being. That's how I felt on Saturday, May 11, 1996, the day I heard Jon Krakauer had disappeared . . . **Had I sent him to his death?**
>
> ~BRAD WETZLE, "SOMETHING HAPPENED"
> **"**

but those on the South Col responded infrequently and could give little information when they did. Helen Wilton, Rob Hall's Base Camp manager, made a list of names and checked them off as climbers were reported safe. Her list showed 17 people unaccounted for, a number that wouldn't be clarified until the next morning.

"Rob's situation was the only one we really knew about," Paula said, "and all night I'd been thinking that he would never stay behind with someone and not have somehow tried to *move*. He knew the danger of remaining stationary at that altitude." Every climber within radio contact had exhorted Hall to come down, assuring him that a rescue team could be sent for Doug the following day.

"It was shocking," Audrey recalled. "Here was a situation where a guide would have to leave behind a still-living client. I remember thinking it would finish him as a guide, and that he was in an impossible situation—damned if he did, doomed if he didn't. Even more shocking was the total lack of news about the 17 climbers who should have returned to their tents on the South Col."

After midnight, Mike Groom and Neal Beidleman, guides for Hall's and Fischer's teams, stumbled into Camp IV on the South Col with two of Fischer's clients and two Sherpas. In a state of near-total exhaustion, they described to Anatoli Boukreev, a Russian

---

FLASH FORWARD "MAKALU" GAU MING-HO

Makalu Gau had to have his fingers, nose, and parts of his feet amputated after spending the night in the death zone in 1996. After undergoing some 15 reconstructive surgeries, he relearned how to walk. He returned to the world of climbing in China in 1998. In 2007, he returned to Everest to lead an expedition up the north side of the mountain for the Taiwan Mountaineering Association. He gives an in-depth account of his harrowing night on Everest in David Breashears's documentary film *Storm Over Everest*.

1996: **Determined climbers—perhaps Doug Hansen and Mike Groom—near the summit late in the day on May 10.**

climber who was guiding for Scott Fischer, where the other climbers were huddled: Cold, exhausted, and unable to see, five more remained out near the Kangshung Face on the far eastern side of the South Col, about 400 yards away.

Groom, Beidleman, and the others barely made it to their tents. Boukreev, who had returned from climbing to the summit without oxygen, was exhausted, but he went out for the stranded climbers. Unable to find them, he returned for better instructions from Beidleman and Groom. On the next trip he found three clients, not far beyond the point he had reached earlier, and he guided them back to Camp IV. Two were left behind. Boukreev said that he didn't see Beck Weathers. Yasuko Namba, if not dead, was unable to walk. Both were clients of Rob Hall.

THE NEXT MORNING AT BASE CAMP

At 4:45 a.m., Helen's radio went off like an alarm. "Is someone coming to get me?" the crackling voice asked. It was Rob Hall. Helen flew to the radio.

"Doug is gone," Hall said cryptically. His voice was partly muffled by his oxygen mask. It wasn't clear if Hall meant that he had been separated from client Doug Hansen, or that Hansen was dead. Hall, at least, hadn't moved from the South Summit.

Paula called Ed at Camp II and told him to get on Rob's radio. It would be best if a fellow climber, a friend, talked to him. Someone would *have* to get Rob moving.

Ed and other climbers gathered in Hall's dining tent at Camp II. Several times Hall asked "'Where's Andy? He was with me last night!'"

(Continued on page 144)

1996: Climbers in Camp II react to the news that Taiwanese climber Chen Yu-Nan has collapsed while descending.

A DIFFICULT PHONE CALL

It wasn't until midmorning on the 11th that people at Base Camp and Camp II were updated with

have died during the night.

"We didn't know what he was talking about," because Hall's client Jon Krakauer had said that he had seen Andy Harris much lower down, on the South Col," Ed recalled. "Andy must have been up there with Rob and Doug for at least part of the night, Rob didn't give any further clarification about Doug, either."

Ed believes that Hansen could have fallen from the traverse between the Hillary Step and the South Summit, but that it is more likely he made it to the slot Hall used as a refuge near the South Summit, and they spent the night there together; Doug must

news from Camp IV: Andy Harris was missing. Scott Fischer and Makalu Gau were last seen below the Balcony, the ledge at the bottom of the South-east Ridge. "Two bodies" had been identified out-side Camp IV, those of Beck Weathers and Yasuko Namba, who were lying on the South Col.

At least two Sherpas and a doctor on Hall's team had hiked out and removed the snow from Yasuko Namba. One account said that her pupils were dilated but that she was still breathing, though barely. Another said that she was completely inert. They found Beck Weathers to be on the verge of death, and the doctor may have deferred to the Sherpas' judgment that the two could not be revived. They returned to the tents at Camp IV, and it was reported to Base Camp that Weathers and Namba were dead.

At Base Camp it was agreed that Beck Weathers's wife should be notified before she found out through the press. Helen Wilton phoned Hall's office in New

(previous spread) 1996: Guides put in fixed ropes around the Hillary Step even as gale-force winds try to steal it.

Zealand. The office manager called Peach Weathers in Dallas and told her that her husband had been reported dead, and that his body had been identified. It was just after 7 a.m., Dallas time.

In addition to Hall and Hansen, Scott Fischer, Andy Harris, and Makalu Gau had to be somewhere on the upper mountain. But throughout that morning the Southeast Ridge and South Summit remained wrapped in clouds and furious winds, with a wind chill well below zero. The Sherpas at Camp IV were exhausted; getting them to head out from the South Col on a rescue effort took some serious coercing by Wongchu, who was at Base Camp.

Wongchu was also the sirdar for the Taiwanese team, and their Sherpas were on the South Col. Finally reaching them on the radio, he scolded them for staying in their tents. "Get up there, *now,* and look for those people," he barked, trying to sound intimidating. "Remind any Sherpas who remain in camp that I'm going to penalize them the moment they set foot in Base Camp."

> "It is so pleasant to sit doing nothing—and therefore so dangerous. **Death through exhaustion** is like death through freezing—a pleasant one.
>
> ~REINHOLD MESSNER,
> *THE CRYSTAL HORIZON:*
> *EVEREST—THE FIRST*
> *SOLO ASCENT*

Ang Tsering, Hall's sirdar, similarly goaded another group of Sherpas into heading up.

Wongchu later admitted that while on Everest the year before he had dreamed of a goddess; she was smiling, and approached him and hugged him. In the spring of '96 the dream recurred, and the goddess again smiled and approached. This time, however, she turned angry, wrathful. During the climbing season, he mentioned the dream to no one.

DOWNWARD MOTIVATION

Paula was trying to be optimistic but finding it difficult. Even if the rescuers reached Hall and the others, how could they get them down? For the entire morning, she and Helen and Guy Cotter, a close friend of Rob Hall's who was climbing on nearby Pumori when the rough weather rolled in, urged Rob to stay alert, turn his oxygen up, and get going. Caroline Mackenzie, Rob's expedition doctor, reminded him to knock the ice off his mask to get it to work properly. Oxygen would provide him the critical boost of energy he needed to start moving again.

In Hall's Camp II dining tent, Ed and others were also on the radio to Hall. "Several people were saying to Rob, 'Don't worry—we'll get to you!' as if trying to comfort him," Ed said. "But he was far too high on the mountain to be rescued. Paula knew this, too, and she reminded me to be tough with Rob, to motivate him in any way possible. Rob *did* need to worry."

It may have been physically impossible for Rob to stand up and start moving. He would have been uncoordinated and weak after his night on the South Summit, and could easily fall off the

The stretch between Camps III and IV can become impossible to navigate if bad weather conditions obscure the route.

Rime ice can cover climbers as they push up the Hillary Step, making them look like a part of the landscape.

mountain. Also, before he could drag himself down-hill he would have to climb up and over the South Summit, a 25-foot rise. In his condition, this would be a monumental task.

Again and again, Ed pleaded into the radio. "Rob, you've got to get up and go—turn your oxygen on full, then crawl and pull your way up the rope and over the South Summit." He told Hall not to wait for the Sherpas, but to meet them halfway. He tried jok-ing with him. "I told Rob, 'You have to come down at least for your wife and new child, who I hope will be better looking than you.' He laughed and appreciated that. For the most part he was coherent."

Veikka Gustafsson, a Finnish climber on Mal Duff's team, cried during the radio calls, which went on for hours. He wanted to speak to Hall, but simply couldn't. He had first climbed Everest as a client with Hall in 1992, then soloed Dhaulagiri in '93 on

another trip with him. Veikka, Rob, and Ed all had climbed with Makalu together.

By now, Ed and others were also in tears. Ed pulled himself together long enough to speak with Rob, then broke down and turned off the radio so that Rob wouldn't hear him crying.

Helen Wilton called Dr. Jan Arnold, Hall's wife, in New Zealand, and held the phone to the radio. Camp II could hear the conversation.

"Rob sounded like a different person when he spoke with Jan," Ed said. "He became more lucid, and several times told Jan not to worry about him. He was positive and strong. That was when everyone listening in lost it."

"Okay, I'm going to try to get up to go now," Rob said finally. Everyone breathed a sigh of relief.

When Rob radioed again a few hours later, Ed was hopeful, upbeat even. "I said 'How's it going,

1996: The location of Camp IV is all boulders, ice, and hurricane-force winds, making it a lonely place.

of picking up all the frequencies used by other teams. They had climbed to the South Col on the 9th, intending to go for the summit on the 10th. But they had arrived on the Col exhausted, and had postponed their summit attempt.

Paula and others at Base Camp urged Philip Wood-all, Base Camp manager for the South African team, to contact his brother, leader Ian Woodall, who was camped on the South Col. Perhaps the radio there could be made available for the emergency. Ian Woodall refused to help.

"They're on their own up there—exhausted, out of food, out of oxygen," Philip protested on behalf of his team. This didn't sound like a description of a team that was still considering a summit push, and it was clear Philip felt uncomfortable with his brother's

Rob? Where are you now?' And he responded, 'You know, I haven't even moved—my hands are so badly frostbitten that I can't deal with the ropes.'"

David and Ed looked at each other, and the distress on their faces spoke for them. It was clear, now, that Hall would be unable to get up and move on his own.

COORDINATION FROM CAMP II

Others needed help. At Camp II the *Everest* team were preparing themselves for rescue efforts, but they first needed to communicate with Camp IV. Hall's tent at Camp II had a 25-watt base station radio, but the batteries of the one working unit on the South Col were dying.

The South Africans had radios at Base Camp and Camp IV, the only radios on the mountain capable

Lost in a storm on Everest, you are in your own world.

decision. "You can't ask them to give up their radio, their one link with the outside world."

"It was crazy," Audrey said, "the way the South Africans kept viewing themselves as separate from everybody else, as if on some other planet. If they had made an effort to join the community on the mountain, they would have realized that the community could benefit *them* as well."

David told Jon Krakauer to rip open the team's tent on the South Col and grab the batteries. The Sherpas had insisted that the tent be locked, following the theft of the crampons from the foot of the Khumbu Icefall.

With the radios on the Col now working, David wanted to assess the situation there before committing climbers and resources. If they were to rush up the mountain, they could get strung out and create an even more problematic situation. They needed to know exactly what kind of help was needed: clothing, food, oxygen, or rescue.

"I think everyone's right at their limit, now," David reported to Guy Cotter after speaking with Camp

> 66
> Everest is this **microcosm of humanity**—warts and all, but beauty and all, too . . . It brings out the absolute best in humans and the absolute worst.
>
> ~JAKE NORTON,
> IN "THE STATE OF
> EVEREST"
> 99

IV. "People are exhausted and hypoxic, and they're having trouble getting up and moving. There's a lot of will up there, but there's a lot of fear, too. We're trying to organize some fresh people to head up with supplies, but on our way up to Rob, for instance, how do we pass by Scott Fischer and Makalu Gau and others who may be in equally dire condition? This may be a triage situation."

CAMP IV IN SHAMBLES

Earlier that morning, May 11, Todd Burleson and Pete Athans, who had spent the night at Camp III, bravely set out for the South Col. The Lhotse Face was being hammered by high winds, and even those who stayed in their tents at Camp III feared being blown off the mountain.

As far as Todd and Pete knew at the time, 17 people were still unaccounted for, but near the Geneva Spur they passed a haggard and frostbitten group of climbers coming down. After receiving pieces of news about others on the South Col, Pete and Todd continued on.

Pete was appalled by the condition of Camp IV. "Our fears were confirmed," he said. "We saw gear strewn to the elements and the torn walls of tents flapping uselessly." They heard voices from one fairly intact group of tents. Inside, Jon Krakauer and another of Rob Hall's clients relayed what they knew. They said that the bodies of Beck Weathers and Yasuko Namba were lying at the edge of the Kangshung Face, several hundred yards away.

Pete and Todd went to work. David had told them to take whatever they needed from the team's tents, which were filled with oxygen and supplies for their own summit attempt.

1996: At Camp II the morning after several climbers died, David and Ed radioed Rob Hall to entreat him to move.

"David just gave freely of whatever was needed," Pete said, "with no idea whether he'd get anything back. Oxygen, for instance, is expensive to replace; without it, his team could lose its chance for the summit."

Everyone on the South Col was inside their tents, and most were too tired to get out of their sleeping bags—even to find nearby oxygen bottles. No one had been strong enough to assist anyone else, and there was no communication even between tents, though many were no more than five meters apart. The Sherpas—those who hadn't returned to the mountain to search for missing climbers—were exhausted, and some were disoriented.

"It was a scene from a horror movie," Pete recalled. "We had to get them down, but some of Rob's members didn't want to leave the Col without him. Only by busying myself with helping others was I able to suspend my incredulity and make the scene appear less surreal."

Pete and Todd encouraged those who were ambulatory and not overly tired to get off the South Col. "We began by delivering bottles to various tents, like pizzas," Pete said. They placed oxygen masks on several climbers, and gave them liquids and nourishment.

The climbers on the South Col were sinking into a dangerous condition of apathy that Todd and Pete found reminiscent of K2 in 1986, when seven climbers trapped by a storm delayed too long on the Shoulder, which at just below 26,250 feet is about the same height as the South Col. When the weather eased, only three of them were able to make a break for Base Camp, and one of these died on the way. Five perished.

The winds were blowing a consistent 70 to 80 mph, with higher gusts, and a half-mile-long plume trailed from the Balcony. The Sherpas high on the

David, Robert, and Ed were climbing the Lhotse Face to Camp III when the news about the Sherpas was relayed to David, who was a hundred feet behind Ed. Ed stopped and cried.

"At that moment all of us, I think Rob included, knew it was over for him. David told me that I'd better say goodbye. But what do you say?—'hang in there'? The last words I had spoken to Rob were that I'd see him on the South Col. Perhaps it was best to leave him with that thought. I simply couldn't have said goodbye, even if the radio were in my hand."

"Our sense of hopelessness was profound," David said. "Rob was only 4,000 vertical feet from us, but we might as well have been trying to rescue the Apollo 13 astronauts. There's no force in nature that can get you up the Lhotse Face and Southeast Ridge fast enough, and there's no helicopter rescue at those elevations. Very few people have survived a night out above the South Col, and the common feature of the nights when they did was that the wind dropped."

After hearing of the Sherpas' abandoned rescue attempt, Hall kept his finger on the radio. David, Ed, and Base Camp could hear him crying. Guy Cotter told him that someone would try again tomorrow.

"Rob said that he couldn't last another night," Ed said. "He knew. But then he quickly turned it around and said, 'Okay, I'll hang in there and be all right.'"

REFRESHMENT AT CAMP III

David, Araceli, Robert, and Ed continued climbing to Camp III. When they arrived, they worked with

> 66
>
> We saw each other, but did not see. We felt each other, but did not feel. We knew each other was safe, but **we knew nothing.**
>
> ~LUTE JERSTAD, ON BEING 27,450 FEET ON THE SOUTHEAST RIDGE
>
> 99

THE SHERPAS TURNED AROUND

At about 4 p.m., Lhakpa Tsering and Rob Hall's climbing sirdar, Ang Dorjee, descended to the South Col. They had climbed to within 800 feet of the South Summit—still two hours away in those conditions. They left some oxygen and a ski pole at the highest point they reached.

On the South Col, Ang Dorjee sobbed as he recounted their efforts to reach Hall. Standing almost stock-still while leaning into a wall of constant wind, tears streamed down his contorted face. Simply watching him was emotional for Pete, who was also despondent.

Todd radioed that one group of Sherpas had reached the Southeast Ridge, but had turned around in the battering winds.

As far as Todd and Pete could determine, the South African team remained in their tents the entire time they were on the Col.

mountain had yet to return to the Col, but Todd and Pete could see that it would be virtually impossible to rescue Hall.

Lines force climbers to stop moving at high altitudes.

1996: Too high on Everest too late in the day, members of Scott Fischer's team descend around 4 p.m.

Winds threaten to blow the 1963 team off the mountain.

unblinking. He hadn't responded when they gave him oxygen and hot fluids.

The afternoon of May 11 was fading. Anyone alive now would likely be dead by morning, after a second night out above the South Col. Anatoli Boukreev began to gather oxygen bottles, aware that he was the only one with the strength to make another try at rescuing Fischer. Pete, Todd, and most of those on the radio from Base Camp were discouraging him, assuring Anatoli that no one would criticize him if he didn't go. Accidents and losses can be compounded when climbers are tired, anxious, and hypoxic. "When rescuing in extreme conditions," Todd said categorically, "you must become very objective—and very calm."

"And at the top of your list is self-preservation," Pete added. "If you don't make it down, neither will the victim."

But at Base Camp, Paula was trying to console Ingrid Hunt, Fischer's team doctor, who was sobbing hysterically, pleading for Boukreev to try to reach Fischer. Haltingly, Hunt described for Boukreev where a syringe of dexamethasone, a steroid that is beneficial for cerebral edema and believed to temporarily increase strength, had been stitched into Fischer's jacket. He should jab Scott in the leg with it.

Moments later, at about 4:30, Todd was standing outside his tent, speaking with Boukreev. Fifty yards away, to his total astonishment, he saw an apparition: A climber was staggering toward camp, straight into a 60-mile-per-hour wind.

"As I went toward him, I could see that his pile jacket was open down to his stomach, his eyes were swollen shut, and his arm was locked upright, parallel to his shoulder, like a mummy in a low-budget horror flick," Todd said. "His face was so badly frostbitten that he was unrecognizable. Then I realized it had to be Beck."

Beck Weathers, the climber described as dead or near dead by both a Sherpa and a doctor, had stood

other guides there to set up a way station, and began heating water for cocoa and soup. Before long, the stream of exhausted climbers that Todd and Pete had passed filed down from Camp IV, some of them on oxygen. The team removed the climbers' crampons, got them into tents, and began warming and rehydrating them.

"I was looking at the face of despair," David said after speaking with several of them. "There was an uneasy mix of elation that they were alive and a sense that something terrible had happened." Many had minor frostbite on their faces. Ed and Araceli got them up and headed toward Camp II before they could cool and stiffen up; if one rests when exhausted, it is difficult to get moving again.

"During this time we were all focusing on Rob and the survivors climbing down," Ed continued. "But Scott Fischer and Andy Harris were out there too, and what were they going through?"

Shortly after the first group of Sherpas returned to the South Col, Ngawang Sya Kya and two other Sherpas also descended. They were assisting Makalu Gau, who was barely ambulatory and appeared to be badly frostbitten.

They had found Gau and Fischer not far from each other, little more than 1,000 feet above camp. Ngawang Sya Kya said that Fischer was barely breathing and that his teeth were clenched and his eyes fixed,

up and walked into camp. Todd and Pete looked at each other as if they had seen a ghost, then quickly put Weathers in Scott Fischer's tent, resigned to the fact that Fischer wouldn't return. Weathers's right arm was frozen solid and felt like a piece of ivory, they said, and he looked near death. They were concerned about his chances of a heart attack: When a deeply hypo-thermic person is rewarmed, they are at risk of a fatal cardiac arrhythmia when the cold acidotic blood returns from the extremities to the heart.

Todd and Pete got Weathers into two sleeping bags and turned his oxygen to full flow—four liters per minute—then administered fluids and brought him hot water bottles. "Beck was exhausted to a degree that I'll probably never know," Pete said.

Todd transmitted the news about Weathers's reawakening to Base Camp. "I can believe anything, now," he said, "and if this guy lives, I bet he'll believe anything, too."

In Dallas, Peach Weathers received another phone call, again from New Zealand, four hours after the previous one. "I didn't register the part about him being in serious condition," she said later. "I just heard that he was alive, and I knew at that point I would see him again." Her brother had already boarded a plane and was flying from Atlanta to help with arrangements for Beck's memorial service. A wake had been turned into a celebration.

> **"**
> When climbers don't take part in the decision making, they are **no longer agents in their own fate** and forsake an intimate connection to the mountain, its weather, and its dangers.
>
> ~DAVID BREASHEARS,
> *THE CALL OF EVEREST*
> **"**

At Camp IV, Anatoli Boukreev was galvanized. "Now I'm definitely going up—Scott's alive, *too*," he announced.

"At that point, I could have believed it," Pete said. "I admit, when I first saw Beck I figured it must have been Scott."

Pete and Todd decided to stay with Weathers, while Boukreev packed some gear and headed up, at 5 p.m. He returned to Camp IV well after dark, and confirmed that Scott Fischer was dead.

The news was met with shock at Base Camp. Ingrid Hunt threw her radio in despair. It crashed on the glacial scree.

A FINAL RADIO CONVERSATION
Around six that evening, May 11, as Rob Hall was beginning his sec-ond night on the South Summit, he again talked to his wife. "Sleep well, my sweetheart," he said to her before signing off for the last time. Audrey said that from the tone of Hall's voice—and against all odds—people almost felt they would be speaking with him again in the morning.

"Our radios were still on, and we continued to talk to him," Ed said, "though we knew that to survive another night was next to impossible. Here was an intelligent, thoughtful person, realizing he was going to die. Earlier, he said he was shivering uncontrolla-bly, but toward the end his senses were dulled and he was apathetic, which is what happens in extreme

---

FLASH FORWARD **SEABORN "BECK" WEATHERS**

Weathers returned home in 1996 and worked hard to recover from his extensive injuries, which required ten surgeries. He spoke about his experience in David Breashears's documentary film *Storm Over Everest*. In 2010, he published a book about his experiences during the Everest disaster and his recovery called *Left for Dead: My Journey Home From Everest*. With the help of an assistant, Weathers still practices medicine in Texas and gives motivational speeches. Though he no longer climbs high mountains, he has become a licensed pilot.

"THE HANDS OF A DEAD MAN"

Quickly, I had to prepare to treat two critically ill climbers who were being led down to Camp II. I would be dealing with their complex medical problems at an altitude where tying your shoes can be confusing.

Makalu Gau arrived with all of his fingers and toes frozen. I used a scalpel to cut away a piece of sock stuck to his foot. He had the worst frostbite I had ever seen—until I saw Beck Weathers.

I had expected an incoherent, half-conscious phantom, but Beck walked in mostly under his own power. In an easy, conversational tone he said, "Hi, Ken, where should I sit?" He was alert and coordinated, showing no signs of hypothermia. We laid him down on a sleeping bag and replaced all his clothes, which were wet down to his underwear.

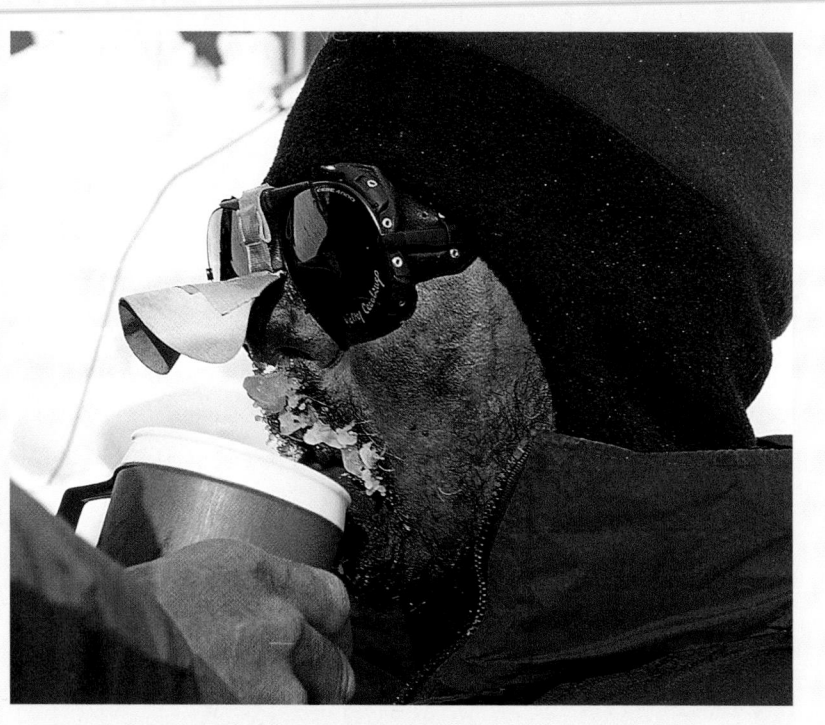

1996: **Beck Weathers was left for dead not once, but twice.**

When I removed his oxygen mask, I was shocked. Edema had swollen his face to twice its normal size. His cheeks were black and his nose looked like a piece of charcoal. His right hand, a third of his forearm, and his entire left hand were deep purple and frozen solid. They radiated cold. There were no blisters, no pulses, no sensation, and no pain. They were the hands of a dead man, but bizarrely, he could move his fingers: The live muscles in his forearm were able to pull on the dead bones in his hand.

I started an IV and injected nifedipine, a drug that diverts blood flow to the extremities, but can cause a sudden loss of blood pressure. Having no pressure cuff, I had to monitor him by feeling the strength of the carotid artery pulsations in his neck. His hands were placed in tubs of water heated to 104°F, but they were literally blocks of ice, and cooled the water rapidly. Maintaining the temperature required continually drawing off the cold water and adding hot water from a thermos. The Sherpas were eager assistants and quickly got the hang of it.

As I worked, Beck talked casually. If you had simply heard the conversation and not seen what was going on, you would have thought he had just dropped by for tea. Beck and Makalu were under control, but I stayed up all night with my two patients, changing their IVs, adjusting their oxygen, and watching them breathe.

At 7 a.m., we heard a discouraging radio message that the rescue helicopter could not come above the Icefall because of the wind. This left me with a hard decision: either wait out the wind at an altitude where even minor cuts won't heal, or descend to Base Camp, exposing Beck and Makalu to further cold and trauma. I opted for the over-the-ice evacuation.

Beck could walk, but Makalu's feet were frozen and he had to be carried. I was so engrossed in how I would manage them at Base Camp that I didn't notice that the wind had died down. I was startled back to the present by the sound of a helicopter overhead.

1996: Climber and physician Ken Kamler treats Beck Weathers's badly frostbitten hands in Camp II.

cold. He was not in pain. When he turned his radio off, he lay down and fell asleep. In those conditions, death is a relief."

A SECOND NIGHT ON THE COL

Only a few at Camp IV knew that Beck was alive. They presumed he would be dead by morning, or in any event would be unable to walk—which was as good as dead. Carrying him down from the South Col would not be possible. That evening, there was some confusion over who would be looking after him. Weathers remembers being alive on the South Col, but alone and in great distress. "During the night I had some water bottles, but because my hands were frozen I couldn't get to them, and I couldn't get anyone to help me. Then I noticed that my arm was swelling, but it was constricted by my cheap plastic watchband, causing loss of circulation in my right hand and lower arm."

At one point, a Sherpa poked his head in the tent, but his English was poor and Weathers couldn't communicate his desire for water or to have his watch removed. In the pitch dark, he unsuccessfully tried to gnaw the watchband off.

In the meantime, gale-force winds were blowing the tent over on him, similar to what other climbers on the Col were experiencing, so he rolled on his side in order to create a space to breathe. Some time before sunrise, the tent door blew inward, and the tent quickly began to fill with snow. When it finally became light out, he began yelling for anyone who might happen to hear.

"Jon Krakauer stuck his head in the door, and he was surprised as hell," Weathers said. "I asked him

1996: Barely able to use his hands, Beck Weathers (third from right) is led down the mountain from Camp III.

if he might be able to get Pete Athans." That's when Pete and Todd prepared Beck to descend. It was the morning of May 12. Fortunately, the wind had subsided somewhat.

HAVING ARISEN, HE DESCENDS

Beck drank a liter of water and sipped at some soup. Although he was having trouble seeing, he was able to walk—haltingly, and with assistance. Pete and Todd had assumed Beck's feet were frozen, and hadn't removed his boots because they wouldn't have been able to get them back on his feet once they had thawed and swelled. However, unlike Makalu Gau, whose feet were badly frozen, Beck was wearing a new model of mountaineering boot insulated with high-tech materials.

Pete radioed Ken Kamler, a doctor on his team at Camp III, that they were bringing Weathers down.

Camp III consisted of a few narrow tent platforms shoveled into a 35-degree slope; there was no room to treat anyone. The day before, Kamler had requested that Base Camp send up medical supplies to Camp II, and after talking to Pete he climbed down in order to set up a field hospital and waited for Beck to be brought down.

Some years earlier, Beck had undergone a radial keratotomy procedure to correct his eyesight. He was unaware that a potential side effect of this procedure was impaired vision in hypoxic conditions. The side effect had only recently been reported in medical journals, and several climbers who had undergone the procedure had experienced no vision problems while high on Everest. The effect, thought to be rare, is always temporary. Additionally, the general swelling of Beck's face from frostbite and exposure had further restricted his vision.

Todd and Pete gave Beck a shot of dexamethasone, which they hoped might improve his strength; put a harness and crampons on him; and started on the traverse to the Geneva Spur. Climbing down the mountain, they had to describe each step for him.

As they left the Col, Pete and Todd looked back briefly, painfully aware that they were leaving their friends Scott and Rob on the mountain. "My emotions can't accept logic as consolation," Pete wrote later. "The image of two shivering, lonely figures, solitary and abandoned, frequents my restless dreams."

Robert and Ed started climbing above Camp III in order to help Pete and Todd with Beck's descent. They met them at the top of the Yellow Band, and the four of them lowered Beck and rappelled beside him. Once Beck was on the fixed lines of the Lhotse Face, he was able to make his way down. His arms were still frozen and he had little coordination, but he had regained partial vision in one eye, with some depth perception.

"Beck became very lucid," Todd said. "He knew he would lose his hands—but he joked about his great disability plan, for instance. When hypoxic, people are often aggressive, fighting you. But Beck was congenial, and he told us to simply 'do what you gotta do.' "

"Beck was quite funny," Robert said in amazement. "He wasn't that depressed. The pathologists in my country, too, are the ones who keep their good humor even in bad situations. In the Alps, I've carried many people down who looked better than he did, and they *died* on the way."

At Camp III, Weathers asked for black tea with sugar. Because he couldn't clutch anything with his frozen hands, he had to be fed.

> **66**
>
> When men climb mountains together, the rope between them . . . is a **symbol of men banded together** in a common effort of will and strength against their own true enemies: inertia, cowardice, greed, ignorance, and all **weakness of spirit.**
>
> ~CHARLES HOUSTON,
> *GOING HIGHER: THE STORY OF MAN AND ALTITUDE*
>
> **99**

"Guys, I'm gonna lose my hands, but I just might see my wife and kids again, if I can ever make it down."

"You can do it," David replied.

"If you think I can do it, I bet I can," Beck said.

At Camp III, David jumped in and helped with the descent of the Lhotse Face. At all times, one of them walked in front, providing support and guiding his feet, while another walked behind, gripping Beck's harness. The anchors for the fixed ropes proved tricky; the climbers had to unclip Beck and then themselves from the rope, and then clip onto the rope again on the far sides of the anchors. Occasionally losing his balance, Beck would reach for the rope, though his hands were unable to grab it.

"I used to tell people that I could do my job with my hands tied behind my back—now I'll have a chance to see if I really can," Beck quipped. He compared their tight group to a conga line, and the climbers joined him in a chorus of "Chain of Fools."

(Continued on page 160)

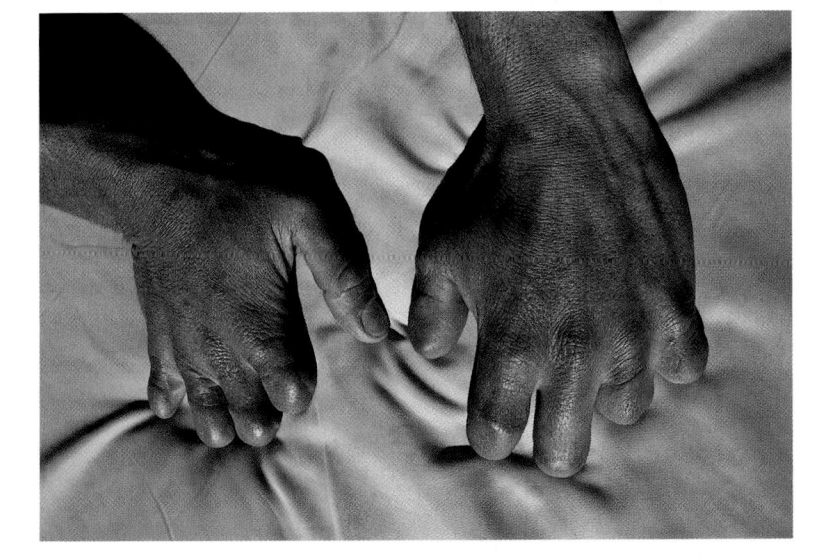

Andy Henderson is one of many climbers who have had fingers amputated due to frostbite from their time on Everest.

1996: **Bundled aboard Madan K. C.'s rescue chopper at last, Beck Weathers gets his ticket to deliverance.**

(previous spread) 1996: Helicopter pilot Madan K. C. struggles to touch down and pick up Beck Weathers and Makalu Gau.

EVACUATION

At Base Camp, Guy Cotter figured that getting a helicopter above the Icefall would almost be possible. But the atmosphere at 20,000 feet provides half the lift for takeoff that is available at sea level, and talking a helicopter pilot into landing near Camp I would be no easy task.

At the bottom of the Lhotse Face, Beck had had to be lowered down the 40-foot vertical wall of the bergschrund. The climbers didn't need to discuss their effort. They had worked together long enough to know exactly what needed to be done. At Camp II, Dr. Ken Kamler took over, helped by Sumiyo, who had also cared for Makalu Gau when he descended.

Cotter had phoned people in Kathmandu who were able to reach the U.S. Embassy. Simultaneously, a group of women in Dallas, mobilized by Peach Weathers, phoned their senators and the State Department. But by the time queries from the U.S. arrived in Nepal, the American consular officer in Kathmandu, David Schensted, had already alerted the Royal Nepalese Army of the need for a rescue.

"I had trekked to Base Camp two weeks earlier," Schensted said, "so I knew the lay of the land up there," which was helpful in discussing the logistics of getting a helicopter to Camp I." He asked for army pilot Lieutenant Colonel Madan K. C. (for Khatri Chhetri), who was related to a staff person at the U.S. Embassy. At 6 a.m. on the 13th, the *Everest* team, Todd Burleson, Pete Athans, a group of Sherpas, and a number of others guided Beck Weathers down from Camp II, while nine Sherpas pulled Makalu Gau in a makeshift sled. They also carried the corpse of Chen Yu-Nan. The other Taiwanese were at Base Camp. All were dreading the extremely difficult evacuation of Gau and Weathers through the Icefall. When they were partway down the Cwm, Base Camp radioed the evacuation team that the wind had died there, and that Lieutenant Colonel K. C. would be attempting to land a French Squirrel helicopter above the Icefall. Few of the climbers were hopeful. But then a miracle took place. While traversing a flat area above Camp I, the evacuation team stopped to watch a small, green object, insectlike and incongruous with the glacier, slowly circle above Base Camp. Then, as they stood in disbelief, the chopper clawed its way toward them with a distant, thwocking rattle.

Ed realized the team had nothing with which to mark a landing spot. "Araceli!" Ed said, "Wait—I have some red Kool-Aid!" She opened her rucksack, pulled out her bottle of Kool-Aid, and tossed it to me."

Lieutenant Colonel K. C. flew above and past Camp I, at 19,500 feet, and continued in the direction of Camp II before turning to descend and attempt a landing. He was alone, having left his co-pilot at Base Camp to make the aircraft lighter. Ed poured out a small X on a flat, 30-meter-wide strip between two crevasses. David dropped to one knee to signal the pilot, and Ed tied a bandanna to an avalanche wand, for a wind sock. The pilot came in slowly and cautiously, clearly uncomfortable with the landing site. As the chopper passed over the deep

It is difficult to fly a helicopter at high elevations, so climbers can't ever take rescue for granted.

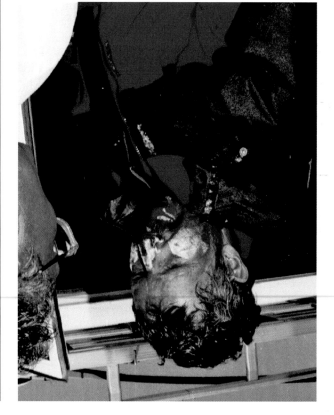

1996: Badly injured but happy to be alive, a safe Beck Weathers talks to journalists about his experience.

crevasse on one side of the landing area, it briefly lost the buoyant ground effect, causing the tail to tilt backward. The protective wire below the tail nearly hit the edge of the crevasse just as K. C. touched the skids to the snow.

He quickly lifted off again.

"Oh no, that's it, he'll never land—his pants are full already!" Robert agonized. But K. C. gained altitude and came in this time from directly above. He never put the entire weight of the helicopter on the snow.

"There was a tailwind, which is the most difficult kind to deal with," K. C. calmly explained later. Gusts of wind at ground level can disrupt the lift and control of the blades, which were already compromised by the altitude. And, if the chopper were to settle into soft snow or a hidden crevasse, the tail could sit back and damage the rotor, causing the helicopter to become lodged.

"Merely getting stuck at Camp I could be fatal to the pilot," said Dr. David Shlim. "Unacclimatized, he

would not live long at that altitude unless he were on oxygen constantly."

K. C. was wearing his oxygen mask, and his attention remained riveted on the controls. With one hand he signaled that he could take only one passenger.

"There was no way I could get into that helicopter and leave Makalu Gau there," Beck recalled. Makalu wasn't able to walk, so his evacuation through the Icefall would be especially hard. Makalu would go. The Sherpas quickly loaded him in behind the pilot.

"At that point, my heart sank," Beck recalled.

The ship hovered upward tentatively, nosed slowly forward, then dropped like a rock out of sight down the Icefall. Lieutenant Colonel K. C. set down at Base Camp and offloaded Makalu Gau.

An interminable 30 minutes passed. Beck looked toward Pete.

"Any guesses on whether he'll be back?"

"The breakfast buffet at the Yak and Yeti Hotel should be opening about the time you get there," Pete answered with a smile.

K. C. returned. "What a tremendous relief that we wouldn't have to carry Beck or Makalu through the Icefall," Ed recalled. He scratched his head and sighed. "It would have taken a day and a night and placed many people at significant risk. K. C. was a 'thank God' kind of guy. For me, the best part of the expedition was Beck's excited, joyful—and slightly incredulous—expression of deliverance." It was one of the highest helicopter rescues in history.

Landing again at Base Camp, K. C. picked up Makalu Gau and the co-pilot, and transported them all to Kathmandu. When they landed on the warm Kathmandu tarmac, Beck was in tears, and patted his bandaged hands on K. C.'s back. He told K. C. how grateful he was and that he knew how much courage it took.

"I had always been told that I was given a brave heart," K. C. said later, "but until this rescue I never had the opportunity to find out if it was true."

No matter how experienced and careful the climber, safety in the Himalaya can never be guaranteed.

CHAPTER SIX

RETURN TO THE DEATH ZONE

The *Everest* team members descended through the Icefall once again and arrived at Base Camp exhausted, frazzled, and shocked. Like those who had returned the day before, some of them cried, finally able to release the anguish they felt over the tragic events. Here, as they removed their crampons, they learned that in addition to the five climbers lost on the south side, three Indian nationals also died below the summit on May 10, climbing on the north side of the mountain.

On the afternoon of May 14, two days after most climbers had returned to Base Camp, more than 60 people congregated at an informal memorial service for the lost climbers, held at the stone lhap-so constructed by Scott Fischer's expedition. The weather was cold and gray. "Only a few days earlier the mood had been one of excited optimism, and now suddenly we were attending a wake," Brad Ohlund observed.

Like most others, he was shocked by the deaths and could only partly comprehend what had happened.

A MEMORIAL SERVICE

Neal Beidleman, Fischer's friend and assistant guide, opened the memorial fighting back tears and paused frequently to weep. Wongchu directed the Sherpas, who ignited juniper branches at the base of the small

1996: This partial cadaver lingered for years off-trail until it was consigned to a crevasse.

rock altar. As fragrant smoke spiraled toward the mountain, the Sherpas chanted prayers. Offerings of biscuits and candy bars were passed around as communion. Rob Hall's sirdar Ang Tsering said, "When I see our good friends die while climbing, this job isn't much good."

Many climbers' hands and feet were bandaged, and they looked like war-zone survivors. Few people spoke until team members, mostly from the Fischer and Hall groups, took turns stepping forward. Some recited poems. Many cried. Some invoked memories of past times, as if reluctant to let go of their friends. "As each victim was remembered, I looked up toward the Icefall and had a feeling that even at this late stage they might come trudging home, down through the seracs—especially Andy Harris, who had simply disappeared," Audrey Salkeld recalled.

Veteran climber Pete Schoening, who had heroically saved several team members on K2 in 1953, offered a moving tribute. Looking much like a grizzled Alaska pioneer in a faded green jacket with fur-trimmed hood, he celebrated Scott Fischer's vitality and ability to inspire others.

"The atmosphere was a bit ominous, and it felt early to be having a service for Scott and Rob," Pete Athans observed, "but a tribute was needed. The gathering of people from all the groups, most of whom had worked together quite effectively, was especially good."

Araceli Segarra offered a European perspective,

> **"**
>
> The **mighty summit** . . . seemed to look down with **cold indifference** on me . . . and howl derision in wind-gusts at my petition to yield up its secret—this mystery of my friends.
>
> ~NOEL ODELL, ON THE DISAPPEARANCE OF MALLORY AND IRVINE
>
> **"**

noting that the memorial was perhaps too open and talkative for something as final as death. "Perhaps this is how it is done in America. They must feel great grief, yes, but we Europeans don't feel comfortable showing our pain to everyone."

"But wounds don't heal when grief and emotions are bottled inside," Paula said.

The memorial marked the last time all of the teams would be together. With the departure of Hall's and Fischer's groups the next morning, the climbers who stayed felt more and more alone with their thoughts and the mountain. As one of them walked sadly over the rubble fields, through the abandoned tent sites, he said he could picture the former hustle and activity, as if the teams were still there.

REFLECTION AND ASSESSMENT

After the ceremony, the *Everest* team retired to the kitchen tent and sat in virtual silence. Over the next few days, as they ate, relaxed, and slept in a relative sea of oxygen, they were able to think more clearly about the recent events and to speak about them. Audrey felt she could hear the words that Colonel Edward F. Norton had written after Mallory and Irvine were lost near the summit on the north side in 1924:

> *We were a sad little party; from the first we accepted the loss of our comrades . . . and there was never any tendency to a morbid*

FLASH FORWARD   **LOU KASISCHKE**

Kasischke has retired from the world of law and business and lives with his wife on the northern shore of Lake Michigan. He spoke about his experience on Everest, including his decision to turn back from the summit, in David Breashears's 2008 documentary film *Storm Over Everest*. In 2014 he published a book called *After the Wind: 1996 Everest Tragedy—One Survivor's Story*, called by a reviewer a "vivid, intimate memoir." He remains active in alpine sports and other outdoor endurance challenges.

blame to individuals—if this were even possible— but to make sense of the catastrophe and to learn from the mistakes that were made. The tragedy, they agreed, resulted from the confluence of bad luck and poor judgment. The guides and clients together had cut their safety margins too thin.

The month of April and the early part of May had seen only one or two full days of good weather high on the mountain. Robert noted that some survivors referred to the weather on the tenth as an unexpected or freak storm. But he and others were not sure the storm was all that unusual. Everest climbers should always be aware of and prepared for such conditions, he stressed.

"The events of May 10 were not an accident, nor an act of God," Jim Williams, a guide, said flatly. "They were the end result of people who were making decisions about how and whether to proceed."

harping on the irrevocable. But the tragedy was very near; our friends' vacant tents and vacant places at table were a constant reminder to us of what the atmosphere of the camp would have been had things gone differently.

News of the tragedy broke in the press and across the Internet. *Newsweek* was preparing a cover story. Liesl Clark of *NOVA Online* reported that the Web site covering the climb received more than 100,000 hits each day during the week that followed the tragedy. "The press accounts, television, and other media reminded us of what happened, which helped us confront our fears, deal with our grief, and heal," Paula said.

Along with friends from other expeditions, the climbers assessed the tragedy, not intending to assign

1996: Looking "like war-zone survivors," exhausted climbers hold a memorial service for their fallen comrades.

Sherpas sometimes set up obstacle courses for clients to practice on before heading for the summit.

South Summit, when one of the climbing Sherpas told him it was still two hours to the summit, Kasischke realized it was time to turn around. Two others on Hall's team also turned around near the South Summit, at 11:30 a.m. The views around them were already blocked by clouds, and they sensed that the weather was changing.

"We felt, because of the bottleneck delay and our 1 p.m. turnaround time, that it was too late to go to the summit, and would therefore be too risky coming back down," Kasischke said. "I didn't rescue anyone, and on summit day did nothing I can take pride in—except that at the critical moment I exercised the personal responsibility that each of us had and made a decision to turn around."

Since the tragedy, the *Everest* team and other Mount Everest climbers have reviewed and dissected the dynamics behind the events of May 10, and the decisions made. No single decision made on the

Unfortunately, not all the guides were really given the leadership or operation protocol for dealing with the various situations that arose on the mountain. The organization was all very loose."

Hall and Fischer had developed a plan to fix ropes high on the mountain well ahead of time. This didn't happen, and led to a situation where difficult decisions needed to be made very quickly. Hall's client Doug Hansen faltered on his descent from the summit, and Hall was faced with an agonizing decision. "Rob chose to stay with his client until he died," Ed Viesturs said. "Had it been me, right or wrong, I might have descended when I realized there was nothing I could do for Doug, even though he was alive. But Rob was a dedicated man."

"I don't believe you can hold any individual responsible for others' deaths. People died because of their own personal decisions," said Lou Kasischke, who was climbing with Rob Hall, just below the

you're in a car crash, an ambulance will pull up and and

"It's a feature of Western society to expect that if death toll in subsequent Everest seasons.

Many have blamed overcrowding for the high true." Hornbein's prediction has proved all too some form." Hornbein's prediction has proved all too happened in 1996 will eventually repeat themselves in business being there in the first place. The events that to get killed helping a stranger who possibly has no obligated to help anyone injured, and I don't want to feel the popular West Buttress of Denali because I'd feel

Dr. Tom Hornbein agrees. "I've written off going to help, and I hope that others will as well."

ation, I'm going to abandon whatever I'm doing to rescuer. When someone is in a life-threatening situ- any high-altitude rescue endangers the safety of the and when they do, everyone is placed at risk because handful of people, some are bound to have trouble, er's chances of success," David explained. "Out of a

"After a point, larger numbers only reduce a climb- tated person at extreme altitudes.

to wait for a slow climber or to rescue an incapaci- climbers don't have a lot of time or reserve strength be available to help if something goes wrong. But numbers—and perhaps assume that someone will parties and individuals imagine greater strength in their push for the top, less experienced groups such as Hall's and Fischer's make at work, too: When large, experienced Brashears identified a "tagalong" factor places such as the Hillary Step, David contributes to bottlenecks and delays at The large number of climbers, however, when breaking trail and fixing ropes. they benefit from extra manpower When multiple teams ascend together,

WEAKNESS IN NUMBERS

lost as a result of compounded factors.

been very different. In the end, lives were storm had come, the outcome might have out of many, hadn't been made, or if no concurred. But if one or two decisions, mountain was necessarily wrong, they

Too many climbers can equal confusion and competition.

save you," added Todd Burleson. "That's not going to happen in the mountains."

Pete Athans and Todd were the only climbers to reach the South Col during the rescue period, fight- ing gale-force winds to get there. Like others who observed the scene on the South Col, they came back humbled. They downplayed their own heroic and lifesaving efforts, and pointed out that the only true rescue was made by the Sherpas who retrieved Makalu Gau from below the Southeast Ridge. "Any- time we try to confront forces of nature so powerful and sublime as those we saw this year on Everest," Pete said, "we realize exactly how helpless we can be, how insignificant are our actions."

INEXPERIENCE

"There were many who seemed confident and brave at Base Camp, like elegant young men and women, yet they took several hours to climb only a short dis- tance," Robert Schauer noticed, "and some of their climbing techniques were awkward and inefficient." One climber pointed out that some of the guides, too, had never been above the South Col. "How could such a person know from experience the types of

(Continued on page 172)

Oxygen is no guarantee of a speedy ascent: Even short distances at high altitude can feel impossibly challenging to traverse.

(previous spread) The Himalaya is a beautiful place, but it can also be dangerous and inhospitable.

TURNAROUND TIME

Even before arriving at Base Camp, all climbers were aware of the importance of descending from the summit in time to reach the South Col before nightfall. The importance of a strict turnaround had been stressed to the guided clients, but on the mountain, these plans were disregarded by all but a few clients and guides.

Ken Kamler had been high on Everest the year before and sensed that Hall, Hansen, and the New Zealand team had stayed high on the mountain too long that year, too. Some team members returned to Camp IV with frostbite.

Lou Kasischke remembered that before he reached the Southeast Ridge in the early morning of May 10, Doug Hansen stepped out of the trail of ascending climbers. When Kasischke passed him, Hansen said that he was tired and was planning to turn around. Instead, Hansen changed his mind and continued upward.

COMMUNICATION

"This tragedy," said Pete Athans, "has certainly reconfirmed the need for a *nonnegotiable* turn-around time, for good support on the mountain, for good reserves of bottled oxygen, and for good communication."

difficult decisions that need to be made, especially at a place like the South Summit?"

Even when using bottled oxygen, climbers get tired enough that they need frequent rests while ascending.

Among those in Fischer's summit party, only Fischer and Lobsang Jangbu, his sirdar, carried radios. Mike Groom, a guide for Hall, had a radio that didn't work. Beck Weathers later pointed out that if the party of his team members that turned around and descended had had a radio, Hall would likely have told him to join them. And if at least one of the lost climbers arriving on the South Col had had a radio, they might have found their way to camp, or their rescue might have been expedited. Tom Hornbein suggests that radio communication, not only between leaders and their guides but especially between leaders of the two teams, would have enabled the leaders to make a collective decision and possibly turn both parties around. With no ability to discuss all the factors at work on the mountain, it is more difficult for a leader to make a unilateral

decision to turn around while another group is still heading toward the summit.

GUIDING WITHOUT OXYGEN

Most guides use supplemental oxygen when guiding at extreme altitudes, knowing that their ability to react to events is improved by the additional mental and physical energy that oxygen provides. On May 10, Lobsang Jangbu was performing many of the duties of a guide, and he summited without bottled oxygen. Anatoli Boukreev, guiding for Fischer, also climbed without it. During his team's summit push, Boukreev spent little time near the clients; after summiting, he descended to the South Col ahead of them. He was in his tent when they became stranded. Although he is rightfully credited for going out later and saving three of them, his decision to

climb without oxygen and leave his clients to fend for themselves has been criticized by many veteran climbers, as well as by Jon Krakauer in his book *Into Thin Air*.

Boukreev, who died in an avalanche on Annapurna in 1997, defended his actions in a memoir called *The Climb*. He argued that if he had used bottled oxygen and it had run out, the shock of losing supplementary oxygen would make him worse off than if he were breathing only ambient air all along. Dr. Hornbein doesn't question what climbers say they experience, but that this argument has no scientific basis. The blunting of judgment that occurs at high altitudes affects veteran guides as easily as it does anyone else. Climbing Everest without oxygen can be rationalized only in terms of personal achievement, not as a safety measure.

Boukreev also explained that he waited on the summit for an hour before becoming cold, a potentially dangerous situation. He thought that by descending in advance of his party he could bring oxygen up to those arriving late on the South Col, though weather prevented this.

AMBITION

An obsession with attaining the summit played an overarching role in the tragedy. Many agree that Hall and Fischer were under pressure to succeed: Clients had paid them substantial amounts to help get them to the top. It might be assumed this would manifest itself in overt pressure from clients, but Yasuko Namba and Doug Hansen were not the type to challenge Hall's advice. Rather, guides placed high demands on themselves to build a record of success in the lucrative guiding business. All climbers were aware that retreating when halfway to the summit would likely necessitate a return all the way to Base Camp, with little hope of a second try.

The press and other media may also have played a role, especially with *Outside* magazine journalist

Climbing without bottled oxygen, alpinist Reinhold Messner summited Everest solo in 1980.

Jon Krakauer and NBC correspondent Sandy Hill (known as Sandy Hill Pittman in 1996) among the clients. With the world watching, and with a corresponding pressure to succeed, it would have been easy for Hall and Fischer to get swept up in a spirit of friendly competition. "It's hard to imagine that it didn't affect Rob to see all of Scott's clients approach and then reach the summit ahead of his, especially after four of Rob's team turned around early," Jim Williams said. The year before, none of Hall's clients had reached the top.

The morning of the summit push, Fischer had left his tent an hour behind the others, climbed slowly, and never managed to catch up with his clients. He may have been suffering altitude sickness—or he may have been just plain sick—and in hindsight should have decided to turn around earlier. "Scott was as strong as an ox, but something happened to him," Todd Burleson said. "It's scary. He has climbed Everest before without oxygen, and now,

with oxygen, he didn't make it back down. This tells me that even as professional guides we're susceptible, that we have to watch ourselves closely, we have to be prepared to turn back."

"Scott was charismatic, good-hearted, and thought well of people—he had a positive attitude that you might call innocently enthusiastic," David Breashears said. "He was as much a cheerleader as an organizer. He may not have realized what utter chaos can occur on an expedition, that situations can arise that seriously test the limits of our control. "Guides and climbers are ambitious, but ambition does not make you stronger," he continued. "It can get you in situations where you shouldn't be. I encountered guides who cheerfully stated, 'Everyone's doing great. We're all going to make it to the top.' And I thought, well, they've reached Camp II. Let's see how they do at Camp III on the Lhotse Face, and then Camp IV. There's a human sort of optimism there, but it borders on the cavalier. On the

Exhausted after his solo sprint in 1980, Messner recovered at Advance Base Camp.

other hand, it may sometimes be good leadership. It's a hard thing to define."

"Unbridled ambition can kill you," Lou Kasischke says frankly. "And it almost killed me. I wish I had never gone to Everest."

SHERPA ASSESSMENT OF THE TRAGEDY

The climbing Sherpas believe that tragic events are not always simple, and that factors such as luck, astrological alignment, and ripening of accumulated karma—along with judgment—play major roles.

Jamling emphasizes that the goddess Miyolangsangma can be defiled by people abusing the mountain—polluting it with garbage or attempting to climb it without proper respect. "The goddess can respond by causing the weather to change, by triggering avalanches or accidents, or by blocking the path down the mountain. I believe this partly explains what happened." Jamling and other Sherpas agree that foreigners are "excused" by the mountain divinities—but only to the extent that they are ignorant of these processes.

Can one really prepare for a wrathful Everest? It is possible to train for Everest physically and to plan for it logistically. But mental preparation, Sherpas recognize, means developing mindfulness and right motivation. A goal can never be reached through force, former Tengboche monk Phurba Sonam points out,

> "
> Everest is a harsh and hostile immensity. Whoever challenges it declares war . . . And when the battle ends, **the mountain remains unvanquished.** There are no true victors, only survivors.
>
> ~BARRY C. BISHOP, "HOW WE CLIMBED EVEREST"
> "

or by aspiration and ambition alone. But if the nature of the motivation is pure, stemming from a compassionate desire to help others, the goal will almost always be reached eventually.

DETERMINATION OF DEATH

Those who set out to rescue the victims and survivors exhibited a large measure of that compassion, and the Sherpas believe the rescuers will earn *sonam*, or merit, for their actions. But victims and rescuers alike have great difficulty in responding appropriately at extreme altitudes, because hypoxia and exhaustion rob them of their judgment.

"I don't think the doctor that looked at me should be faulted for declaring me dead, or close to death," Beck Weathers later said with calm sincerity. "It may not have been the best diagnosis, but we all make mistakes at times, even at sea level. He's an excellent doctor and a great guy, and he was the one climber of many on the South Col who ventured out during a period when there wasn't any great stampede of the cavalry to look for survivors."

Many wonder how Beck could have been identified as dead, when he later stood up and walked away. "Weathers's resurrection complicates the already prickly process of judging a person's medical condition in a harsh environment that only grudgingly gives back life," said Dr. David Shlim.

(Continued on page 180)

FLASH FORWARD   PETER ATHANS

Athans has developed a reputation as one of the world's most experienced high-altitude mountaineers. Called "Mr. Everest," he has climbed the mountain seven times. A 1997 medal from the American Alpine Club recognized his rescue efforts on Everest in 1996. He has worked on film projects, including *Seven Years in Tibet,* and went on a National Geographic expedition to Nepal's forbidden Kingdom of Mustang. He's published *Tales From the Top of the World: Climbing Mount Everest With Pete Athans* and *Danger and Discovery in the Sky Caves of Nepal.*

DEATHS ON EVEREST

Charting the number of fatal accidents on Mount Everest's major climbing routes from 1921 to 2014.

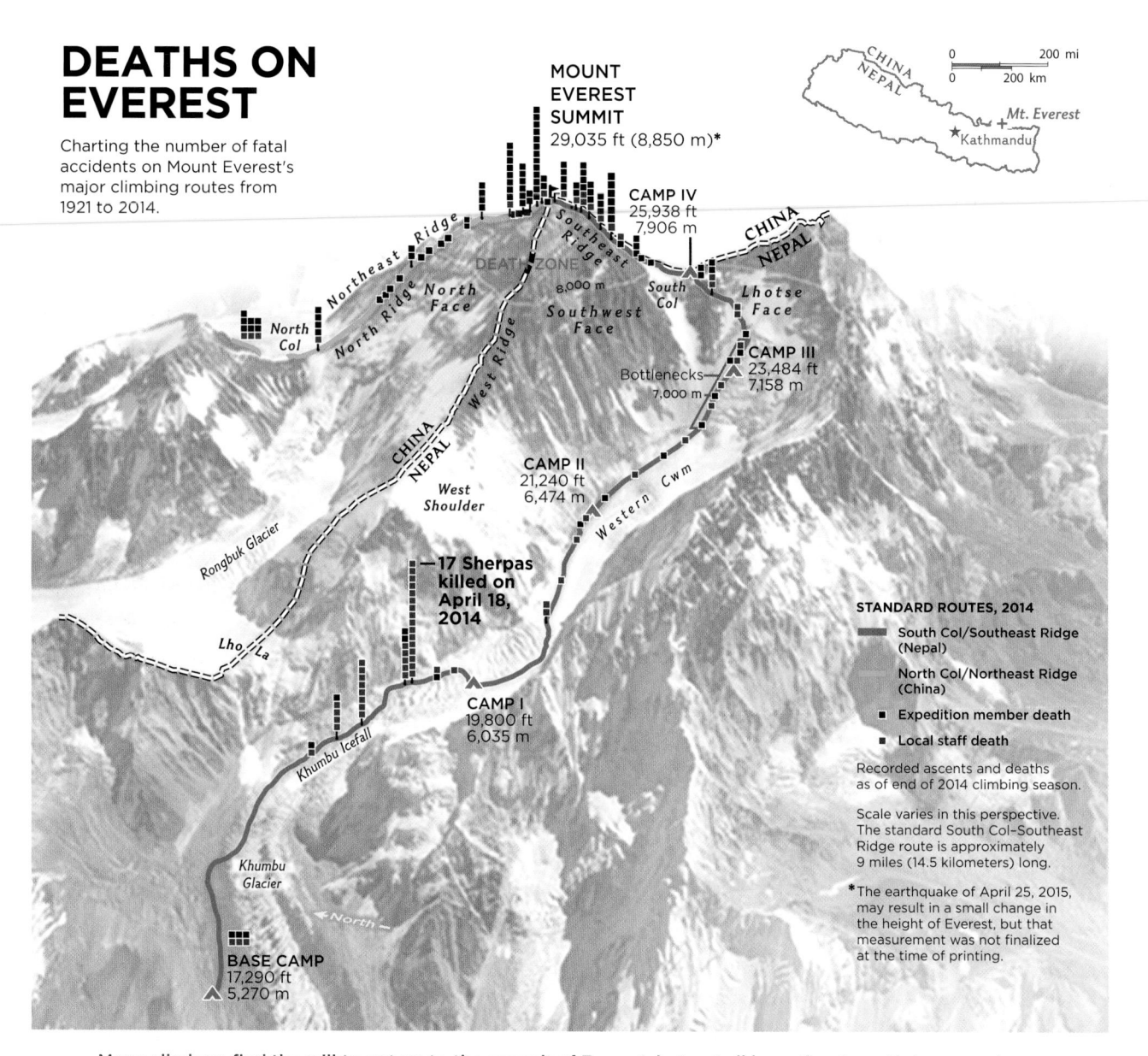

Many climbers find the will to get up to the summit of Everest, but not all have the strength to come down.

Unless Weathers's resurrection is explained as a miracle—and Beck himself doesn't discount an element of the miraculous in his survival and rescue—then surviving as he did must be considered possible for anyone. "The beautiful thing about Beck's recovery is that not all of it can be explained," said Dr. Charles Houston.

What are the implications of Beck's survival in terms of the efforts that should be taken to save others stranded in extreme settings? At present, climbers, medical people, helicopter pilots, and others apply their years of experience and the best of their abilities to rescue the injured and stranded. Should the knowledge that someone may—but more likely may not—be still alive in an isolated, dangerous location inspire already committed rescuers to endanger themselves to an even greater degree?

"The fact that Beck was left for dead and survived is going to haunt rescue decisions for years to come," Shlim said. "But ultimately, those who can be pulled

(previous spread) Climbers ascend into the clouds, which can be thick enough that you can't see the person before you.

to safety will be, while those who appear lifeless, or for whom not enough resources are available, will be left behind."

Yasuko Namba, for example. She died on the South Col near the spot where Beck Weathers lay before he arose. Perhaps Namba—and others before and since—may have had a longer window of survivability than people assumed. She may have been alive on the morning of the 11th, and she was lying only 400 yards across relatively flat terrain from the tents of Camp IV.

The confusion over who should have been caring for Beck Weathers was also unfortunate. Having stunned everyone by surviving the storm and a night alone on the South Col, Beck was then inadvertently neglected in his tent in Camp IV and left to either suffer or die alone. Remarkably, he defied the odds against his surviving a second excruciating night, and was led down to Camp II the next morning.

But the conditions on the South Col are difficult to imagine. Given what the people who went out to check on Weathers and Namba knew, and in view of the frightful conditions, they likely made the most appropriate decision. "Easy though it may be to second-guess them," Charles Houston said, "one cannot fault them for what they decided in their brain-numbed condition."

Diminished awareness and limited judgment is thought to have contributed to many of the accidental deaths on Everest. At 26,000 feet, people simply don't think the way they do at sea level. One of the first symptoms of hypoxia is loss of some mental faculties, especially judgment.

Hallucinations are common under hypoxic stress. "In 1933, Frank Smythe fed a bite of mint cake to an unseen companion, and saw strange flying objects over the North Ridge which his friends jocularly called 'Frank's pulsating teapots,'" Audrey observed. "And Reinhold Messner's companion Peter Habeler had an 'out of body' experience when, floating above his own shoulder, he watched himself climbing the upper slopes."

> 66
> The death toll has been alarming, and **climbers are asking hard questions.** But who will answer them?
> ~CHARLES HOUSTON,
> IN *VOICES FROM THE SUMMIT*
> 99

A TOUGH DECISION

"After the tragedy, I felt very mortal and very humble," Breashears recalled. "The mountain ceased to be a source of joy for me. Suddenly the wind seemed louder, the cold colder, my legs weaker, and the mountain higher. I thought, 'Wow, Breashears, by putting yourself and the team at this kind of risk, you've bitten off more than you can chew this time.' But the death of a close friend on another expedition tends to impact you less than when one of your own party dies. Our group was still intact. I wanted to ruminate for a few days over whether to carry on with our attempt, and to make a decision after talking with the team. Thankfully, there was no pressure on us from MacGillivray Freeman Films to continue."

Ultimately, whether or not to return to the mountain would require a personal decision from each member. Ed didn't want to leave with a pall of gloom hanging over the mountain. He wanted to remind himself and demonstrate to others that Everest can be climbed safely, and even be enjoyable and rewarding. "Everest isn't necessarily a death sentence or some sort of penance," he said.

Jamling's situation was more complicated. His wife, Soyang, and other relatives were opposed to him returning to the mountain; it had been hard enough for him to convince Soyang in the first place. Jamling asked her to again consult Geshé Rimpoche, their family guru and adviser, and request a new *mo*, a divination. Soyang agreed that if the mo was favorable, she would relent.

In Kathmandu she told Rimpoche about the tragedy and the weather, and Jamling's desire. He again consulted the beads, then gave her his answer.

(Continued on page 184)

LIKE RUNNING ON A TREADMILL AND BREATHING THROUGH A STRAW

1996: **David Breashears helps a young monk at Tengboche view his monastery's entryway through the camera.**

More than 280 people over the years, including many excellent climbers, have perished on Everest, tumbling from cliffs, being swept away by avalanches, or succumbing to exposure, exhaustion, or altitude sickness. Many of the bodies are still up there. In 1985 I collected body parts from two climbers who had died the year before. Their corpses had frozen solid on the mountain and shattered when they fell to the glacier below.

In a dark and mysterious way, the deadly nature of the place has only strengthened Everest's grip on the world's imagination. Because the dangers are so obvious, Everest has come to symbolize for many people the ultimate in personal ambition and achievement. Thomas Hornbein, who took part in the first American ascent, in 1963, once described climbing Everest as "a great metaphor for human striving, myth, and the world that is a part of all of us." This explains, in part, why otherwise rational people will pay handsomely to tag the top.

Even veteran Himalayan climbers like myself can find ourselves firmly in the mountain's grip. The risk of death is enticing, because it reminds you that you are alive. "The fact that either you or one of your companions may have the possibility of dying," Sir Edmund Hillary once said, "not only

doesn't stop you doing it, but it's almost one of the things that keeps you going." But for me, it's also about the cold, the fatigue, and the challenge of good climbing. It's about the way snow crunches on a minus 10°F morning but squeaks on a minus 20°F morning. It's about moving around a corner and seeing the pink granite of neighboring Makalu glowing in the first rays of dawn.

Everest has this immense psychic gravity that pulls you into its orbit. When George Leigh Mallory and the British reconnaissance team of 1921 set out to find a route up the mountain, it was no more than a set of coordinates on a map. The hulking monster they discovered came as a surprise. "Suffice it to say that it has the most steep ridges and appalling precipices that I have ever seen," Mallory wrote to his wife, Ruth. "I can't tell you how it possesses me." Three years later, climbing from the Tibetan side, Mallory and his partner, Andrew Irvine, disappeared into the clouds near the summit, never to be seen again.

I remember as a boy taking a book off the shelf in my family's apartment and turning to the famous photograph of Tenzing Norgay standing on the summit. Something fused in my 11-year-old brain as I stared at the Sherpa's thick down suit and overboots, and the ice ax and flags he held aloft in exultation and triumph. I was struck above all by the unwieldy oxygen mask obscuring his face. What kind of place was this, I wondered, where a man needed to carry oxygen to survive?

Today I know the mountain as an environment so extreme there is no room for mistakes. After the May 1996 storm, members of our film team climbed to Camp III to help nearly a dozen survivors and later managed a helicopter rescue near Camp I. Now, back at Base Camp, we were emotionally drained. As we attended an informal memorial for the lost climbers, the summit was flying its pennantlike plume of clouds from the jet stream. At night we lay in our tents listening to the wind on top roaring like a 747 on takeoff. Yet we all knew as professionals that we had obligations to make the film, and we were confident in our climbing skills. We agreed to go back.

Just before midnight on May 22, a dozen of us set out from the South Col, climbing by our headlamps and the dim light of the stars. Climbing above 26,000 feet, even with bottled oxygen, is like running on a treadmill and breathing through a straw. Everything tells you to turn around. Everything says: This is cold, this is impossible. Two hours into the climb, we passed Scott Fischer's body.

Later we found Rob Hall. We kept climbing. By 11 the next morning, we reached the top.

In years to come, I knew, the lessons of the tragedy on Everest would be all but forgotten. Climbers would take the same risks, make the same mistakes, and some of them would die, as climbers have been doing for more than nine decades. But smelling the earth and the fragrant trees above Tengboche monastery days after our summit, I realized in the deepest sense my own good fortune. I had survived Everest once more. I wondered if I would be wise enough to stay away.

1996: **Despite the hardships and the tragedy, Araceli Segarra and Jamling Tenzing Norgay fought their way toward the summit at 27,600 feet. David Breashears was there to capture it.**

Soyang called Jamling and relayed Rimpoche's finding, and from the lightness of her voice Jamling immediately knew the response: " 'Go! Go up! The circumstances haven't changed for you.' "

If the mo had been unfavorable, Jamling said that he would have respected her wish and abandoned a second attempt. He admitted that, were his family not involved, he might have proceeded with the climb anyway, but only after taking additional precautions, by commissioning further pujas, and by making offerings and prayers.

"Doing pujas and obtaining blessings from lamas is important and can be helpful," Jamling stressed, "but the critical element in climbing Everest, for Sherpas as well as foreigners, is having a strong *lungta*, wind energy, and right motivation. These determine our destiny on the mountain and are ultimately within our control. We must exercise good judgment, self-restraint, and respect for the power of nature."

But the period of bad luck wasn't completely over. Nawang Dorje, the Sherpa with Scott's team who had contracted what may have been a complicated case of pulmonary edema, was evacuated to Kathmandu from the Pheriche Aid Post, his condition deteriorating.

The team's climbing Sherpas sat about Base Camp, demoralized and unenthusiastic about returning to the mountain. Some of the Sherpas stopped in to see Pheriche Aid Post doctor, Jim Litch, with vague complaints, though he felt they visited more to get a prescription of hope and confidence. Ever practical, other Sherpas were concerned that the deaths might result in fewer Everest expedition jobs. But guides and Sherpas would soon find that the events of the spring season appeared to have no such effect.

Araceli wanted one more shot, having put so much time and energy into the expedition. But second

> 66
> We felt **the lonely beauty of the evening,** the immense roaring silence of the wind, the tenuousness of our tie to all below. There was a **hint of fear,** not for our lives, but of a vast unknown, which pressed in on us.
> ~THOMAS HORNBEIN,
> *EVEREST: THE WEST RIDGE*
> 99

thoughts crowded in. "I don't want to climb on a route with dead people on it," she said, crying.

"This has been a big shock for me. I've never seen such serious frostbite before, and I've thought a lot about the dead and the survivors," Sumiyo added. "I didn't know Yasuko well; she had climbed the highest peak on every continent, and Everest was her final summit. But this doesn't make me afraid for our team, because I trust each of them. We are strong, experienced, and ready."

"I never thought about *not* going back up," Robert said. "We had a job to finish, and actually felt that the window of calm weather hadn't yet come. The other teams that remained suspected this, too."

It was unanimous: They would try to get as high as safely possible.

Paula Viesturs was unprepared for the decision. She was tired and stressed, and became angry at the first news of it. Ed was certain it would be harder on Paula than on him. The tension at Base Camp had been unrelenting, and she decided to take a walk for a few days, knowing it would be that long before Ed and the team would be high on the mountain again. She hiked down to Tengboche with the departing New Zealanders. She wanted to clear her head, to see the flowers, to decompress.

"The mountain is a place of astonishing beauty," David said expansively. "Despite all the work, the tragedies, and the setbacks, we wouldn't be going up again if there wasn't also a lot of joy in it. Seeing the younger climbers' drive and enthusiasm also helps Ed and me. But none of us are afraid to come home without having made it to the summit."

"As experienced climbers, we have all lost good friends to the mountains over the years," Jim Litch reflected. "In spite of this, we continue to climb. There must be an element of denial that it could ever happen to us; otherwise, how could we knowingly continue to put ourselves at risk?"

1996: **Testament to human frailty and Everest's ferocity, abandoned and wind-shredded tents litter Camp III.**

RESTOCKING THE SOUTH COL

While members of most other teams were headed home, the *Everest* team was trying to find the strength, and the bottled oxygen, to head back up the mountain. During the rescue period they had volunteered their oxygen, as had all except the South African expedition. In order to film, a summit team of 11 to 13 people would be needed, with a budget of four or five bottles per person—a total of 50 bottles. Twenty-eight bottles had been expended on the South Col during the tragedy; restocking the South Col would be at least two days' work for the Sherpas.

Todd Burleson's team had oxygen, but they also planned to make another attempt. Guy Cotter offered to replenish most of the *Everest* team's oxygen supplies, because Hall's team had expended much of their oxygen on the South Col.

THE MONSOON APPROACHES,
BUT THE WIND IS THERE ALREADY

The grumbling and shifting of the Khumbu Icefall was growing, and the route through it was becoming difficult to maintain. Mal Duff's team, which had installed and repaired the route throughout the spring, had departed, but two Sherpas remained to work on it.

On May 17 the team again left Base Camp, and by late morning they topped the Icefall. Again, they plodded into the reflected heat of the Western Cwm and the blinding glare from the layer of smooth, melted snow ahead. Early that afternoon they arrived at Camp II, which had become like a second home. They would wait here for the wind to relinquish its grip on the mountain.

In their tents at night the team heard the ominous roar of wind on the mountain. "We needed calm weather soon, because our climbing permit ran out on the first of June," David said. "But our motivation might have run out first."

If the high winds continued, pushing for the summit would be difficult, and threading film through the camera would be impossible. At the least, they hoped to complete the mission of installing the weather station on the South Col, which Roger had prepared them for.

Base Camp was windy, too. Brad Ohlund estimated the wind speed at 40 miles an hour, and he worried that his tent, with him in it, would get blown, bouncing and tumbling, across the glacier. "For three days my radio inquiries as to how the climbers were doing were answered in the same way," he reported. "'We're cold and tired. We want to get this done and go home.'" The fatigue of a long expedition had begun to set in.

Pete Athans, Todd Burleson, and Jim Williams had also returned to the mountain with two of their five clients. They settled in beside the *Everest* team at Camp II and waited five days before abandoning their attempt. Their clients didn't feel good about the mountain and elected to return home.

"If we had reached the top, having to guide paying clients past the corpses of our friends would have brought little joy," Pete said. "And I have to admit that our decision to retreat was partly influenced by the international news media. With all the attention focused on the mountain, the press would crucify us if a client was harmed, and we could not justify the risk."

Along with the team, a Spaniard, a Frenchman, and Göran Kropp, the lone Swede, decided to remain on the mountain. The South Africans also announced their plan to try for the summit again, which worried some of the climbers on other teams.

By May 20, the reports and satellite images showed that the weather for May 23 looked fairly good. The weather was improving daily, and during the daytime it became hot inside the tents at Camp II. Sitting at 21,300 feet in shirtsleeves, Ed looked ahead to the climb. "We have to assume that not all of our team will reach the summit," he said. "Anything can happen: lack of desire, illness, or other variables that are out of our control. And especially when you've been on the mountain for eight or ten weeks, you're homesick, tired, and have lost weight—and that's right when you reach the higher altitudes and the going gets *very* tough. The climbers who have patience, persistence, and reserves of motivation will be the ones who summit."

From a distance, this image of Sherpas on the West Ridge in 1963 illustrates how precarious the route can be.

CHAPTER SEVEN

"CHOMOLUNGMA HAS LIT A LIGHT WITHIN ME"

On the night of May 20, the team finally received confirmation from meteorologist Martin Harris in England that the jet stream had moved to the north. A window of good weather was opening. David Breashears described the summit plan: "In the early morning of May 23—around midnight of the 22nd—we will leave the South Col and head up.

Four Sherpas will assist with the camera, two Sherpas will carry oxygen for the others, and two will cache additional bottles on the Southeast Ridge for the returning climbers. No Sherpa will carry more than 35 pounds." If all went according to plan, the summit team of 11 climbers and Sherpas would be on top by 10 or 11 a.m., and back on the South Col between 2 and 4 in the afternoon, giving them a safety margin of a few hours before darkness set in. "Keep your fingers crossed and say your mantras," David advised. "Now, we only need that good weather."

TO THE COL

The team then attended to important details such as taping insulating foam to the handles of their ice axes. Gripping steel in minus 30-degree temperatures

1996: **The first light of dawn creeps over a peak to the west of Everest's mighty summit.**

would conduct the cold right into their hands, increasing the risk of frostbite.

On May 21 the team set out for Camp III. When they arrived that afternoon, they crawled into the tents perched on the snow shelves they had dug into the Lhotse Face. Over the past few weeks, they had climbed to Camp III and descended to Base Camp four times.

The next morning they continued upward. At the Yellow Band, known to geologists as the Chomolungma Detachment, the world's highest fault, Ed reminded himself to stop on the way down to collect rock samples for geologist Kip Hodges. The team then crossed the Geneva Spur, and in early afternoon reached Camp IV on the South Col, at 26,000 feet. Araceli was awed by Everest's proximity. "When I stepped onto the Col, I could hear the mountain murmur. It came out in full display—black, white, red, orange, and gold—a magnificent pyramid of rock and ice. The wind had created a different landscape; the spent oxygen bottles, twisted aluminum, and shredded nylon of abandoned tents made the Col look like a field of metallic snow flowers."

The team's storage tent was still standing; despite the high-tech materials used in their construction, tents are often destroyed by the Col's ferocious winds. Yasuko Namba's body was 400 yards away, but two other bodies lay in the open nearby, though no one paid them much attention. Dealing with one's own life here at the lower edge of the Death Zone was more urgent.

David decided that one member of the team should remain on the South Col as a communications and safety officer. With regret he selected Sumiyo Tsuzuki, whose cracked ribs would have endangered her summit attempt.

"I was disappointed, but knew that my role in supporting the team on the South Col was important for assuring their safe return," she said later.

(*Continued on page 194*)

1996: **Sherpa members of the *Everest* team carry loads toward the Yellow Band.**

After setting up camp, the climbers dried out their clothes, mittens, and inner boots, which had become wet from perspiration. By 5 p.m. on May 22, they had finished melting snow and ice for their water bottles and had gagged down a few bites of food.

HANGING OUT IN THE DEATH ZONE

Doctors and Himalayan climbers recognize the Death Zone as a general term, but the dangerous effects of extreme altitudes on the body and mind are difficult to overstate. Above 26,000 feet, climbers generally don't want to eat, drink, put their boots on, or go outside—even the smallest amount of physical exertion requires an arduous effort. The body deteriorates rapidly at this altitude; sleep is barely possible and not restorative; and food is poorly absorbed. Humans cannot survive for extended periods above this height.

(previous spread) 1996: **Despite the emotional toll ahead, Ed Viesturs ascends through the Yellow Band.**

"Araceli put on her oxygen mask and fell asleep immediately!" Ed laughed. "I lay there for four hours remembering how hard it was to climb Everest without oxygen. Had I trained enough? Was I still mentally strong enough? I didn't want to let anyone down, including myself, and was anxious to get moving."

David and Robert had to work that night. Confined with their cooking gear and the film equipment in a three-man tent, Robert had to load four large IMAX film magazines while David checked the camera lenses and body—operations that were complicated by their cumbersome oxygen masks, which they frequently removed. Without bottled oxygen, however, they could function for only 15 minutes before their muscle reactions and movements slowed down.

At Base Camp, Paula was nervous. "I still have dreams and fears about Ed climbing. I've trained myself to be positive, and I practice envisioning Ed and the rest of the team standing on the summit and getting down safely. Each climb is a new situation, a new mountain, and I believe in our team's ability to make the right choices." Paula, Liz, Brad, and Wongchu decided to get some sleep, but it was a restless night.

THE CLIMB

At 9 p.m. on May 22, Ed arose, melted more snow for water, and forced down a Pop-Tart, the last solid food he would consume for 48 hours. Knowing that he wouldn't eat on the mountain, he added some energy drink to two liters of water and placed the bottles in his pack.

It can take seven liters of water a day to remain fully hydrated at high altitudes, but climbers can't carry that much. Despite their dehydration, they experience little thirst and are too cold to think about drinking the half-frozen slush in their water bottles.

"I woke Araceli, called Paula on the radio, climbed out of the tent, and told David that I'd see him soon," Ed recalled. He left an hour before the others, at 11 p.m. Climbing without oxygen and breaking trail, he expected that the rest of the team would catch up with him.

The sky was black. Ed tried to remember from his reconnaissance the day before how to skirt the crevasses of the steep ice bulge above Camp IV. "Probably by sheer luck, I hit the fixed rope at the bottom of the Triangular Face right on," he said. The rope led 800 feet up a snow gully, at a 30- to 40-degree angle, then onto a snow slope at 50 degrees. It was slightly windy, typical for early morning on the mountain. Paula's words over the radio echoed in Ed's thoughts: "Climb that mountain like you've never climbed it before."

He climbed methodically, kicking through the fresh snow. He looked back occasionally for the headlamps of the rest of the team. His breathing was rapid. Step . . . pant . . . step . . . pant . . . Each laborious step took five seconds, a pace that slowed as he gained altitude. Though the walking distance from the South Col to the summit is only a mile and a half, the climbers can cover the terrain at an average of only 12 feet per minute.

By now, David and Robert had broken ice into a pan and "brewed up." They put on their overboots and placed water containers and two oxygen bottles in their packs, along with still cameras, spare mittens, spare goggles, and a couple of candy bars. They checked the pressure on the oxygen bottles to make sure they were full, and rechecked the regulators to confirm that the oxygen was flowing at a rate of two liters per minute. They clipped on their crampons and had a sip of tea before leaving. At midnight they joined Jamling and Araceli outside.

"While we lay in our tents, she didn't stop puffing," Araceli wrote of the wind high on the mountain. "But before we left the Col she became quiet, as if consenting to our climb."

> 66
> By climbing mountains we were not learning how big we were. We were finding out how breakable, **how weak and how full of fear** we are.
>
> ~REINHOLD MESSNER, IN "HOME ON THE RANGE"
> 99

FLASH FORWARD ANG DORJEE SHERPA

In 2002, Ang Dorjee immigrated to the United States to join his wife, whom he met at Everest Base Camp, and began his work as a wind turbine mechanic. They now have two children and live in Amsterdam. Ang Dorjee returns to the Himalaya every spring to visit family members in Nepal and to climb mountains as a guide with Adventure Consultants. He has now summited Everest 17 times and made 28 ascents of 8,000-meter peaks. He has guided climbers up not only Everest but also Africa's Kilimanjaro and Argentina's Aconcagua.

The four went off into the darkness, their visible world defined by the reach of their headlamps; deep breathing and the crunching of crampons on the ice were the only sounds. Jamling felt the coolness of his mother's ivory rosary around his wrist. He chanted mantras while counting off the beads between his thumb and the crook of his forefinger.

The Sherpas also were ready to depart the Col, and they radioed Base Camp to check in. A Sherpa at Base Camp lit a juniper incense fire at the lhap-so. He would keep it burning until the entire team returned to Camp IV.

TO THE SOUTHEAST RIDGE

Ed was making better time than he expected. "The knee-deep snow was a hassle, but it was exciting to be up there and I resolved to plow through it." After two hours of climbing, the beam of his headlamp illuminated a corpse, sitting upright. The face and upper body were covered with snow. It was Scott Fischer. "I found it hard to look at him," Ed recalled sadly. "I wanted to spend some time there, and decided that I would stop on the way down."

In the South Gully, just below the Southeast Ridge, Ed realized that the rest of the team wasn't catching up, so he dug a hole in the snow, sat down, and waited. Without bottled oxygen, he quickly became cold, and after waiting for 45 minutes he decided to move on. He waited again on the Balcony, at 27,600 feet, the first landmark of the Southeast Ridge. He was exhilarated to be so high on the mountain, witnessing the first glimmer on the horizon grow brighter and bathe the world in amber light.

The rest of the team plodded upward. "On summit day, I'm in a cocoon," David said, describing the final push. "I get into a mantra of rhythm, and every bit of focus and ambition goes into putting one foot in front of the other. I feel reduced to elemental thoughts, to a state of consciousness that emanates from the need to survive. It's not a creative mode.

Climbers sometimes rummage through the cast-offs of expeditions past at cluttered Camp IV.

1996: **The team pauses in oxygen canister–ridden Camp IV, which Barry Bishop once called the "world's highest junkyard."**

I become pragmatic and methodical, and monitor my body's functions and resources. With every step, I'm thinking about my pace, my breathing, my posture, the time frame for reaching the Southeast Ridge, and the weather—wondering whether, once we reach the South Summit, we will still be a group, with Robert and the camera somewhere nearby."

To stay warm, Ed had to keep climbing, and he continued to push through knee- and thigh-deep snow. David, Robert, Araceli, and Jamling waited at the Balcony for the IMAX camera, and were joined by Jesús Martínez of Spain, Göran Kropp of Sweden, and two Sherpas. Thierry Renault of France, climbing on the South Africans' permit, was ahead of them. "As we waited and watched the sun rise, I turned off my oxygen, but took a few lungfuls every ten minutes to stay warm and active," Robert said.

Araceli was excited. "I felt euphoric when we reached the Southeast Ridge—partly because I was sharing that beautiful day with the people on our team. We had a good attitude and knew we were finally on our way to the top."

Jamling sat and observed the tiny flat spot below the Balcony—his father's and Sir Edmund Hillary's last camp before the summit. He remembered the story of his father's night there on the snow shelf barely large enough for a small tent. Jamling then gazed out over Khumbu, placid in the morning haze far below them. He felt he could hear the ritual chanting of monks, their pulselike drumbeats and high-pitched horns.

When Jangbu arrived at the Balcony with the camera, David and Robert set up a shot. They promptly realized they had lost their voices—not uncommon at altitude—from deeply breathing the dry, cold air through an oxygen mask, which dries the air even more. They communicated with each other in sign language.

From the Balcony, the team started on the 1,100-vertical-foot ascent to the South Summit.

By the time they reached it, they had been moving continuously for nine hours.

THE SOUTH SUMMIT

"At 9 a.m. a voice croaked over the radio," Liz Cohen reported, who was at Base Camp, "and we all jumped out of our seats. David and Ed were at the South Summit, and the rest of the team trailed behind by at least one hour." The two waited there for some minutes before they became cold, then continued on. At that altitude, the simple act of breathing requires so much metabolic energy that it is not possible to stay warm for more than a short time—regardless of clothing.

Just beyond the South Summit, David and Ed came upon Rob Hall's body. "It was obvious that he had done all the right things," David said. "He had surrounded himself with extra oxygen bottles and removed his crampons to help keep his feet warm. He had applied his formidable willpower and mountaineering skill in a heroic attempt to survive. But Rob was a long way from help. Nobody could have survived in those conditions, and nobody could have saved him."

"Seeing Rob Hall's body was the hardest part of the ascent," Araceli said, "and he was right at a place where we most needed to concentrate—not a place to make a mistake."

They were now only 300 vertical feet from the summit, but had yet to surmount the treacherous Hillary Step. In *Tiger of the Snows*, Audrey recalled, Tenzing Norgay described the winding "snowy humped" ridge of the South Summit and the steep, rocky step—later termed the Hillary Step—some 40 feet high, that blocked his and Hillary's progress in 1953. Hillary discovered a vertical crack in the outcropping and was able to get into it and jam and wriggle his body upward. Tenzing followed.

> 66
>
> What do we do when we reach the summit? **We weep.** All inhibitions stripped away, we cry like babies. With joy for having scaled the mightiest of mountains; with relief that the **long torture of the climb** has ended.
>
> ~BARRY C. BISHOP, "HOW WE CLIMBED EVEREST," 1963
>
> 99

As David moved ahead, he could see that the route up the Hillary Step had changed and was more awkward and time consuming than in 1983 and 1985. Also, the route was laced with a confusing and entangling maze of old fixed ropes. Thierry Renault was ahead of David but moving slowly, spurring fears of another delay.

For Araceli, everything seemed to go wrong at the Hillary Step. Her nose started to bleed and she stopped, holding up climbers behind her. Then, when she placed her handkerchief inside her oxygen mask, her goggles fogged. "After I finally climbed the Hillary Step, I asked Jamling how far it was to the summit," she said. "Of course he hadn't been there either, but the summit ridge seemed to go on forever."

SUCCESS

At 10:55 a.m. Nepal time, May 23, Ed radioed Base Camp to say that he and David had gone as far as they could. "From where we are now, it's downhill in all directions," he announced from the summit. The Sherpas heard cheers from the dining tent and came in to join Liz, Paula, Brad, and Wongchu.

Jangbu caught up with Ed and David on top, and the three of them waited 20 minutes for the camera. Climbing sirdar Lhakpa Dorje was also moving slowly, having decided to climb without oxygen. Again, Ed was getting cold and had to get going—which meant descend. He passed Jamling and Araceli as they approached the top, and gave them each a hug of congratulations.

Around 11:35 a.m., Jamling, Araceli, Robert, and Sherpas Lhakpa Dorje, Thilen Dorje, and Muktu

(Continued on page 202)

Stephen Venables looks triumphant at climbing the Kangshung Face, even after a night at 28,000 feet.

1996: An exuberant Jamling Norgay strikes a top-of-Everest pose.

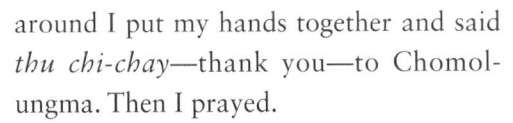

around I put my hands together and said *thu chi-chay*—thank you—to Chomolungma. Then I prayed.

"I prayed that my father might be able to watch and be proud, and I prayed also for our safe descent."

Alternately facing in the cardinal directions, Jamling cast small handfuls of blessed rice into the air. He then unfurled the long prayer flag and tied it to the cluster of other flags and katas adorning the metal survey stake anchored in the summit snow by an Italian expedition.

Jamling then struck his father's summit pose for the camera, not realizing that his stance was the reverse of that now famous image of Tenzing. He was connected by radio to his wife, Soyang, in Kathmandu, who was nearly breathless. "Now, no more!" she exclaimed and reminded him to be cautious coming down.

He placed the photographs of his mother, his father, and His Holiness the Dalai Lama on the summit, along with the packet of blessed relics from high Tibetan lamas. Next to the photographs, Jamling left the rattle from his daughter.

When the IMAX camera arrived, David began filming. He kept his oxygen mask on almost constantly, in order to concentrate better, and shot one 90-second roll of film. "Having already climbed Everest, my main goal was to get the camera on the monopod and fire it up," Robert said. "When I heard the sound of the camera operating smoothly, I was thrilled, for this was an important reason we came to Everest."

"We accomplished something historic, and it was a wonderful moment," David said. "But I was also concerned that everyone get down as safely as they got up."

Jesús Martínez reached the summit around 12:35. With him was Ang Rita, who had now climbed Everest a record ten times. Accompanying them was

Lhakpa reached the top. Araceli took out the Catalan flag while Jamling and David took photographs of her. Over the radio she was connected to a reporter with Catalan television, and she declared that she was hungry for more chocolate.

Jamling may have been the most ecstatic. "The moment I reached the summit I felt a rush of excitement. This was where my father had stood 43 years ago. I hugged David and thanked him, because he had given me the opportunity to climb Chomolungma. I cried a bit out of joy, and as I looked

(previous spread) 1996: Looking up from the Southeast Ridge, the IMAX *Everest* team progresses toward the summit.

Thierry Renault, climbing with two Sherpas, and Göran Kropp, who was very tired. It was Kropp's third attempt that season.

A DIFFICULT DESCENT

Ed was moving downhill quickly. "At the South Summit, I sat down with Rob and just talked. He was on his side, and his left glove was off." Hall's wife, Jan, had asked Ed to take photographs of Hall's body. Viewing those photos later, Ed and David saw something that Ed hadn't noticed when he took the shot: a piece of material sticking out of the snow a short distance from Hall that looked as if it could have been covering a knee or an elbow. It may have been Doug Hansen, who was assumed to be near Hall, attached to the fixed rope.

> 66
>
> One fast move or a moment of inattention and our bodies would have remained **down a crevasse forever.**
>
> ~EDMUND HILLARY,
> IN *VOICES FROM THE SUMMIT*
>
> 99

Lower down, at 27,000 feet, Ed again sat down, and he asked Scott Fischer about what happened. David, too, was affected strongly. "Scott was in a very lonely place, and it was sad to see him there. In another hour he'd have been in camp."

Neither Ed nor David was able to move Hall's or Fischer's body away from the route. "Rob's wife, Jan, and Scott's wife, Jean, had asked me to try to retrieve some remembrances from them," Ed recounted. "Rob wore a watch, and Scott wore his wedding ring on a thong necklace. But it was too immediate and too personal for me; I couldn't disturb them. I had always thought I'd grow old with them, and assumed that if they got in a situation like this one, they'd come through

1996: **Despite lagging behind Ed by about two hours, other members of the *Everest* team soldier on.**

it alive. I'd never had a close friend die anywhere, let alone in the mountains, and here were two good friends—dead. Their faces were covered with snow—thankfully, because I wanted to remember them as I had known them. Alive."

On the descent, Araceli became lethargic and eventually sat down, unaware that her oxygen had run out above the Hillary Step. "It felt awful and dangerous," she said. Robert had to prod her into standing up and moving.

Jamling was at their cache of reserve oxygen bottles at the South Summit, and he put a new bottle in her pack. "'Wow! Oxygen again! Let's go!' was how I felt," Araceli said. "Jamling and I sped—*vroooom*—down the mountain. When we arrived at the South Col, three hours later, Jamling told me he had set the

> ❝
> I have climbed my mountain, but I must still **live my life.**
> ~TENZING NORGAY
> ❞

regulator at three liters per minute flow. I said, 'What? So that's why we were going so fast!'"

"The South Col no longer seemed a cold and lifeless place, and I was happy to arrive there," Araceli wrote in her journal. "The wind had stopped, and I turned and looked at the upper mountain. She stood elegant and powerful; an air of kindness surrounded her, or maybe it was my own sense of peacefulness at having stepped safely onto her icy skin." Araceli and Sumiyo hugged, and Sumiyo gave her tea. The team then collapsed in sleep.

David was relieved. "For me, the day wasn't joyful until the moment all of us were on the South Col and in our sleeping bags. We were rewarded for our patience and perseverance, and were graced with two days of fine weather.

Chortens honor Sherpas and climbers who have perished.

ED VIESTURS, HVR, AND VO$_2$ MAX

"Ed has a rare ability to operate exceedingly well at high elevations," said David Breashears, a powerful climber himself.

"Ed chose his parents well," explained Dr. Robert "Brownie" Schoene, a pulmonary critical care physician and expert on high altitude medicine. "Much of his ability is due to his genetics. But anyone who has climbed with Ed will tell you that he simply moves well. He's smart and careful, but bold enough to do great climbs."

Since the late 1970s, Dr. Schoene, an accomplished mountaineer, has studied the performance capabilities of endurance athletes and high-altitude climbers, and was a member of the 1981 American Medical Research Expedition on Everest. Before Ed departed Seattle for the *Everest* Film Expedition, Schoene tested him at the University of Washington's Pulmonary Function and Exercise Laboratory. Predictably, Ed scored high on every test.

To determine his response to hypoxia, Ed relaxed as he breathed into a mouthpiece that measured the quantity of air he exhaled. Over ten minutes, the amount of oxygen supplied to him was decreased, causing hypoxemia, or a low level of oxygen in the bloodstream—which in turn stimulated his breathing. Ed's "hypoxic ventilatory response," or HVR, ranked high, meaning that the volume of air he breathed increased substantially as the oxygen supply was decreased.

"At moderate altitudes of 10,000 to 14,000 feet, where the available oxygen is only 60 to 70 percent that of sea level, a brisk HVR minimizes the susceptibility to some high-altitude illnesses and may improve performance," Schoene said. "But above 20,000 feet, where there is very little excess oxygen, adequate breathing is essential to insure that enough oxygen gets from the lungs to the blood and into the tissues."

On the summit of Everest, about 30 percent of a climber's oxygen intake goes to the physical activity of breathing. "This means that 30 percent of the climber's energy is spent simply on survival," Schoene said. "At sea level, a normal person at an

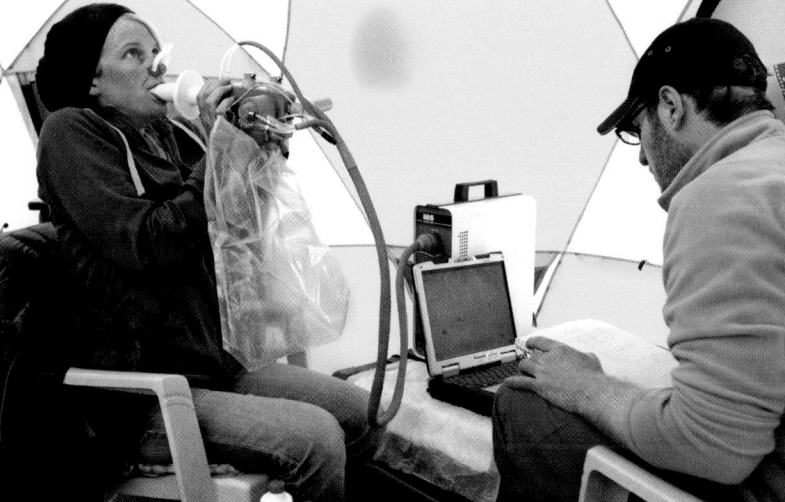

Studies continue: Climber Emily Harrington's lung capacity is monitored during National Geographic's 2012 Everest expedition.

exhaustive level of exercise spends only 7 percent of his energy on breathing."

Aerobic capacity, or "VO$_2$ max," by comparison, is the maximum volume of oxygen an individual can absorb at the end of exhaustive exercise, and is a marker of aerobic fitness. Schoene and others have determined that low-altitude endurance athletes have a high VO$_2$ max. Ed's VO$_2$ max tested very high. "People then assume that elite extreme-altitude climbers must also have huge VO$_2$ max levels, because as one ascends, the ease of oxygen consumption falls," Schoene pointed out. "But some climbers defy this, particularly Reinhold Messner, the first person to summit Everest without supplementary oxygen. Messner's VO$_2$ max is higher than the norm, but is not exceptional. The relationship between VO$_2$ max and climbing ability is somewhat of a mystery."

Other factors also enable Ed and other successful extreme-altitude climbers to move well in the mountains, such as an efficient biomechanical makeup. But following the tragic deaths of May 1996, many people have brought up the idea of testing climbers—especially guided clients—before recommending they climb Everest.

It's been a hard expedition for me. Standing on top was an anxious moment because of those we know who stood there less than two weeks before us, but didn't make it down. I'm ready to go home and relax."

"Ed did a great job breaking trail," Robert said, "and it's amazing that he did it without oxygen. All night we saw only a tiny white spot moving well ahead of us—that was Ed." He smiled with satisfaction. "We formed a nice community and had good relationships all around, like brothers and sisters—even though those don't always work!" he said, laughing.

"That night, I would have liked to enter the minds and dreams of everyone there," Araceli wrote later. "The Sherpas, giving thanks to the divinities that protected them . . . Ed thinking of Paula; probably that night they both would sleep . . . David and Robert reviewing each of the decisions and steps they made, and finally feeling happy, congratulating each other . . . Jamling, traveling the path of his childhood memories, warm from the summit dream that the gods had granted him . . . and Sumiyo, navigating the sadness of returning home without achieving her dream, but with her strong soul planning her next summit . . ."

The team was grateful for Sumiyo's support, and she was happy that they had returned safely. "Now,

> 66
> Yes, it is a **graveyard.** It also is a **monument** to will, courage, discipline, self-reliance, individuality, responsibility, ambition and achievement . . .
>
> ~JOHN MEYER, "WHY WE CLIMB: IF YOU HAVE TO ASK, YOU WON'T UNDERSTAND," 1996
> 99

I look forward to getting away from this small tent and narrow sleeping bag, and to having a hot bath and fresh bedsheets. That is my wish!"

All of them shared excruciating memories of their friends, so recently alive. "This experience might now provide me with a signpost that says, maybe you'll be smart enough to stay away from the mountain for the rest of your life," David remarked, though his eye retained its customary twinkle.

THE HIGHEST WEATHER STATION

The next morning the South Col was clear. Araceli slept soundly, and Ed had to shake her to awaken her. The team managed to fight their exhaustion and hypoxia to break camp, then assemble the GPS device and weather station.

In slow motion, they hauled the instruments over to a fairly remote site. They plugged the six sensors into the recording system and used camera tripods to support the anemometer, which indicates wind speed and direction. A separate tripod held the temperature sensors and telemetry antenna. The team deployed the solar panels and then anchored all the parts with rocks.

Then they set up the GPS device, pointed it properly, activated it, and took measurements. The data from the GPS would be used to determine changes in the position and elevation of the South Col since a year earlier, when

---

FLASH FORWARD   **NEAL BEIDLEMAN**

Beidleman returned to the Himalaya in 2000 to attempt to climb Annapurna with Ed Viesturs, Veikka Gustafsson, and the editor-in-chief of *Alpinist* magazine, Michael Kennedy. They were forced to give up the attempt due to avalanche risk. He returned and successfully summited Everest in 2011, in part to make peace with his experience there in 1996. He reflects on his 1996 experience in the documentary film *Storm Over Everest*. He works as an engineer and photographer in Aspen, Colorado.

measurements had last been taken. From this data, Roger Bilham would later calculate that the South Col is rising at 4 millimeters per year and moving toward India at 18 millimeters per year.

In 1996, Roger said that he hoped the weather station they installed would "tell us about the weather high on the mountain and, with proper evaluation, make the mountain somewhat safer for climbers." Ever since, weather stations in the region have indeed provided new data on the unusual monsoon alpine desert setting of Mount Everest. In 2011, the Italian Ev-K2-CNR Pyramid Network installed a weather station on the South Col—making it the highest weather station in Khumbu. This station takes hourly measurements of temperature, humidity, atmospheric pressure, wind speed and direction, global radiation, and precipitation.

Although a weather station could be placed on the summit, it is difficult to secure anything to the very top of Mount Everest because the ice that builds up in the winter is ablated and blown away in the summer. "Also, mountaineers hope they are achieving something at the edge of human limitations when they reach the summit," Roger added. "It could be disappointing to find a weather station there."

RETURN TO BASE CAMP

Jamling wasn't able to help with the weather station. When he returned to the South Col from the summit, he had napped briefly, then awoke to realize that he was snow-blind. Snow blindness, caused by too much ultraviolet light from the sun—usually exaggerated by reflection from the snow—results in conjunctivitis-like irritation of the cornea. During the climb, Jamling's oxygen mask had fogged his snow goggles, and for much of the climb he hadn't used them.

1996: David Breashears captures the summit scene on camera.

"That was the most frightening moment of the climb for me—how could I go down? I tried eyedrops, and Sumiyo helped, but I had to break camp and stuff my pack with my eyes closed."

By morning, Jamling could open his eyes for a few seconds, but they quickly teared up. Climbing sirdar Lhakpa Dorje helped him toward Camp II. "On the Lhotse Face, I'd steal a glance for anything dangerous above me, then look down at the route and plunge ahead with my eyes closed. I prayed and thought of my father." He improved at Camp II. Jamling mentioned the pain only in passing, though snow blindness is acutely painful.

"Returning to Base Camp was a celebration for me," Araceli said. "Some drank beer, but I'd been dreaming about Coca-Cola. I ate so much chocolate that I was too full to eat dinner. Alone in my tent, I thought about all we had done, and I cried, happy that we were safe."

The day the team left Base Camp, May 29, the Sherpas and climbers gathered at the lhap-so and again stoked the juniper incense fires. Along with

at Base Camp found it difficult to congratulate the South African team members who had returned.

A HERO'S WELCOME

"Araceli! Araceli!" chanted an enthusiastic crowd as Araceli Segarra, the first Spanish woman to reach the top of Mount Everest, arrived at El Prat airport in Barcelona on June 9. Besieged with attention, she was received by the president of Catalonia, Jordi Pujol. "I was delivered fan letters addressed simply "Araceli, Alpinist of Everest, Spain." Looking as though she had stepped from a health club, she joked, "I got more rest at Base Camp, where I could sleep without the phone ringing all the time! I lost my voice telling and retelling the story of the expedition. Although some reporters wanted to hear only of the deaths, it was a relief that people in Spain weren't as aware of the May 10 tragedy as in the U.S. When

the team members, they gave thanks to the gods for granting them safe passage, and prayed that they be granted an opportunity to return. They then lowered the *thar-chok* prayer-flag pole while a former monk read a prayer. Base Camp had become uncharacteristically quiet.

But another tragedy was about to occur. That day, after the very late hour of 5 p.m., Bruce Herrod, a British climber with the South African team, radioed from the summit. He was never heard from again. Herrod's was the 11th Everest death of the season. Brad Ohlund was outraged. "How could the South Africans not have learned from what happened just a few days earlier? I'm angry that they allowed a climber to summit so late, and let another person die." The surviving members of the South African team passed through Base Camp on their way down. There were a few nods and hellos, but those still

1996: Araceli lolls at Camp IV the morning after her ascent, her mind and body still feeling the ill effects.

something safe and successful happens, nobody cares, but I tried to convey the good sides to our story."

A PARADE IN DARJILING

A third of the way around the world from Spain, Jamling also received a hero's welcome. "In Kathmandu," he said, "Geshé Rimpoche and Chatrul Rimpoche gave me a rare collection of sacred objects to keep on my altar, which will continue to bless me and my family." From there, Jamling left for India, and several hundred relatives and friends greeted him at the border between Nepal and West Bengal. They draped katas around his neck and fed him tea and biscuits. Signs were plastered across the front of several cars, welcoming him home.

The winding streets of Darjiling, about an hour away, were graced with banners. Jamling was paraded through the hillside town to his family home, where a crowd of Sherpas bearing katas greeted him at the threshold. They also presented him with welcoming *chema*—rice and tsampa held in a divided, ceremonial tray. He took pinches of each and flicked them into the air, as is done at wedding receptions. Beer and chang flowed. "They made me finish an entire bottle of beer before I could enter my own house." A warm welcome evolved quickly into a great party.

"The Darjiling Sherpas were proud of me and proud that I'd advanced my father's name, but mostly I had made them proud of themselves. They were glad that I had been successful on Everest and in America, yet had decided to return to them, to my roots."

Jamling went straight to the altar in the chapel room. His father's thangka scroll painting of the goddess Miyolangsangma rests prominently on the altar, and he did three prostrations, a way of

> **"**
> So for those who wonder, 'Why do they do it?' . . . I can remember what I would have said before May 10: To climb the great mountains is to leave the comfort of familiar places and to **challenge the very essence of oneself.**
>
> ~PETER HILLARY, "EVEREST IS MIGHTY, WE ARE FRAGILE," 1996
> **"**

concluding the prayer for good luck and safe travels that he had recited when he departed the house. "I believe that the success and overall safety of our expedition can be partly attributed to the prayers, pujas, lighting of butter lamps, and audiences with lamas," he said thoughtfully. "I feel more devout than I did before the climb. Chomolungma has lit a light within me."

He admitted that his high-altitude mountaineering goals were now largely satisfied. He had climbed the mountain for himself and to pay homage to his father, and would now remain at home with his wife and child in Darjiling, running the trekking and climbing business started by his father.

Following his Everest expedition, Jamling joined 350,000 other devout Buddhists in Salugara, West Bengal, for a Kalachakra ("Wheel of Life") initiation presided over by His Holiness the Dalai Lama, who personally blessed him, Soyang, and his daughter.

(Continued on page 213)

Edmund Hillary, Tenzing Norgay, and expedition leader John Hunt enjoyed great fanfare when they arrived at Heathrow airport in 1953.

SHOULD EVEREST BE GUIDED?

In 1985, David Breashears accompanied Dick Bass, 55, up Everest, the first guided summit. Since then, several Everest clients have cited Bass's success as their inspiration. Breashears, however, points out that Bass was not average; he carried his own loads and climbed without ropes where even some experienced climbers have difficulty. "Dick is very independent-minded—he's a powerhouse, a force of nature," Breashears says respectfully. "But for others," he adds, "reaching the top is like stepping up to the plate in the ninth inning of the World Series and hitting the ball out of the park—without having trained, season after season, to acquire the skills needed to get there in the first place."

"The ability to pay the $65,000 fee doesn't make you more experienced," Robert Schauer concurs, expressing a legitimate apprehension about novice clients. But clients come in every variety, from unseasoned trophy seekers to experienced Himalayan mountaineers looking for an outfitter and a permit. It should also be remembered that three of the five climbers who died on the south side of the mountain on or shortly after May 10 were experienced guides. "These deaths did not result from the actions of clients," says client Lou Kasischke, who turned around just below the South Summit.

Kasischke points out that if everything is going right, Everest is very climbable. But if anything goes wrong—and mistakes can be made easily and quickly by even the best—people will die. It is virtually impossible for guides to save anyone above the South Col. After Camp IV, the time for "coaching" from the guides is over.

And guides are not paid to take risks. They are paid for their judgment of what risks are worth taking. Indeed, in the mountains, a climber's judgment and attitude are critical. Three of Rob Hall's clients, acting on their own judgment, avoided a life-threatening situation when they decided to turn around.

"Sometimes, climbers will put every bit of their physical and psychological energy into reaching the summit, leaving it to the guides, and others, to get them down," Pete Athans says.

Athans points out that the clients pay him to make his best decisions, but that sometimes means denying them the summit. His associate Todd Burleson concurs: "I feel it's better to have everyone come home safe, but disappointed, than to have one person die." This kind of decision making, in fact, is what most clients are looking for.

"Climbing is no longer only a sport; it has become a business, and for some their only income," concluded Charles Houston. "The more ventured, the more gained." He suggested that this gamble might explain the risks that some guides and clients—possibly for different reasons, and against high odds of weather and terrain—are willing to take on a dangerous mountain such as Everest.

"I consider myself a cautious mountaineer," David Breashears says. "I don't like to take unnecessary risks, and because of that I might live longer. You can't forsake yourself, or others, for the summit of a mountain."

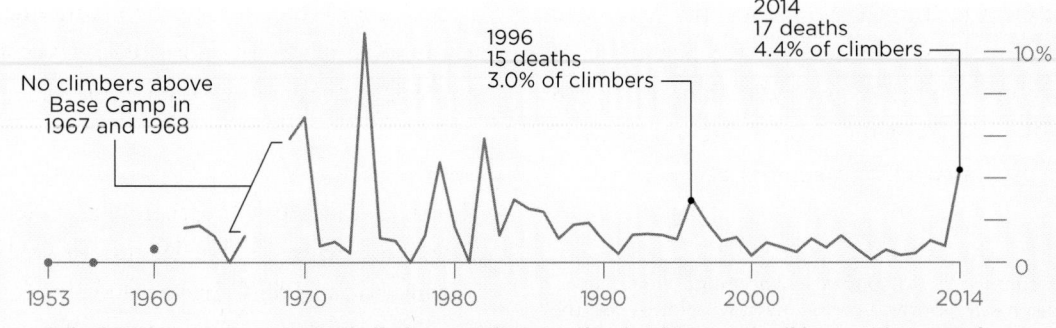

Calculated as a percentage of climbers on Everest, the death rate overall has not increased.

Adventurer Göran Kropp, who climbed Everest in 1996, holds an armload of climbing gear.

For a period of time while the team was on the mountain, Robert's family and office staff in his Austrian hometown of Graz had been in a panic. The headline of an Austrian paper had just reported "Styrian Climber Lost on Everest." The article referred to an unnamed mountaineer lost in a tent at 27,000 feet on Everest. As it turned out, an Austrian from Robert's home province of Styria had died on the north side of the mountain, but the climber's identity was not confirmed for almost two days.

When he departed Austria in March, Robert had told few people that he was heading for Everest. He was concerned that press accounts might raise expectations about his success and create unwanted pressure. He returned to Austria with no fanfare and enjoyed a week of private time before the press found him and coverage of his climb appeared in the media.

Göran Kropp had also accomplished something of a first—he had completed what was certainly the most self-sufficient combined approach and climb of the mountain. David remarked on the conviction, purity, and innocence of the Swede's approach. On his first, solo attempt, Kropp had turned around when he encountered high winds and deep snow near the South Summit, agonizingly close to the top. His irrepressible enthusiasm was unaffected, and he cheerfully recognized that he would have to accept some assistance and a climbing partner for his two subsequent summit pushes. Kropp said that he intended to bicycle home by a different route, through Russia.

Jamling was in Darjiling during the fall of 1996 when he heard that Lobsang Jangbu, Scott Fischer's climbing sirdar, had died in an avalanche that swept three climbers from the Lhotse Face. "Lobsang always sought Geshé Rimpoche's blessing before he climbed. But Rimpoche passed away in July, shortly after our spring climb, so Lobsang climbed on Everest in the fall season without Rimpoche's benediction. He was killed on that climb."

In Kathmandu, Elizabeth Hawley, the renowned Everest statistician, informed Robert Schauer that his 1996 climb—when compared with his ascent 18 years earlier—marked the longest interval between any individual's two Everest summits.

LIFE BEGINS AGAIN

Shortly before Beck Weathers was evacuated from Everest on May 13, Dr. David Shlim, Director of Kathmandu's CIWEC Travel Medicine Center, heard reports that Weathers's arms were frozen up to the

(previous spread) 1996: Congratulatory hugs greet the conquering heroes of the *Everest* team when they return to Base Camp.

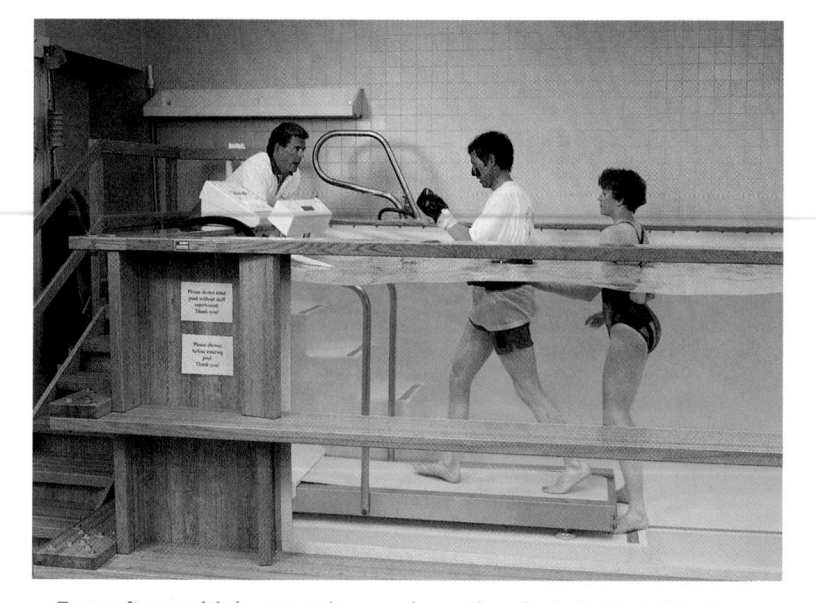

Even after multiple operations and months of rehab, Beck Weathers would be forever changed by his miraculous survival on Everest in 1996.

elbows. "But when Weathers arrived at our clinic, it was remarkable how good his overall condition was," Shlim said. "Here was the guy I'd been hearing about for two days—first as confirmed dead, then as too ill to risk trying to rescue. And then 24 hours later he walked into my clinic unassisted."

Makalu Gau was in the main examination room downstairs, unable to walk because of his frostbitten feet, so Shlim settled Beck into the exam room upstairs. First, Beck wanted to call his wife. Shlim dialed the phone for him, and Beck chatted warmly with a very happy and relieved Peach Weathers.

"Most impressive was Beck's charm, concern for others, and lack of concern for the media," Shlim said. "Initially, he refused interviews, stressing that the real story was the guys who walked him off the South Col and Lhotse Face—Todd, Peter, Ed, Robert, and David."

But a month after Beck returned to Dallas, it became evident that no function would return to his hands. Surgeons there performed state-of-the-art microvascular surgery to save as much of his arms

> 66
> The line between success and disaster is razor thin, and only **seen clearly in hindsight**.
> ~NICK CLINCH, PAST PRESIDENT OF THE AMERICAN ALPINE CLUB
> 99

as possible, and he was given skin grafts. Nevertheless, his right arm was dead to his watchband—the one he couldn't gnaw off his arm—necessitating that the arm be amputated in mid forearm. The fingers of his left hand were dead to the knuckles, including the thumb. Surgeons cut the web of skin between the stump of his thumb and the rest of his hand, giving him limited opposition. He can lay the thumb sideways against his hand and perform tasks such as picking up a piece of paper.

Beck's nose was also destroyed by frostbite. Using cartilage from his ears, some skin, and a piece of rib, doctors rebuilt his nose upside down on his forehead. Once the blood supply was established, they rotated it into position.

In place of his right hand, Beck wears a myoelectric prosthetic device that reads electrical currents from the muscles of his forearm to open and close a claw, allowing him to pour a cup of coffee and pick it up. "When I first wanted to make this trip," he joked, "I looked at the outrageous cost and said, 'You know, this thing is going to cost me an arm and a leg.' Well, as you can see, I bargained them down.

"Once you've been dead, everything looks pretty good for a while," Weathers said softly. "But it doesn't get much better than coming home to your family. The price that I paid is one thing, but the price my family paid is another. I was able to come back and tell them everything I hadn't been able to before, about how much they mean to me."

"Beck has an incredible will," David said in amazement. "He knew he would lose most of his hands, but he just decided that he wanted to live. He's our one miracle, the one great inspirational story out of all the tragedy—along with the selfless heroes among the climbers, Sherpas, Base Camp staff, and the helicopter pilot who gave their all to the rescue."

A HEROIC PILOT

As head of his Royal Nepalese Army squadron of helicopter pilots, Lieutenant Colonel Madan K. C. felt that if anyone should try a rescue at Camp I, he should. Although most of his flying missions in Nepal are rescues, K. C. said that few survivors have thanked the pilots, and none have written letters. Peach Weathers was an exception, and the letters she wrote poignantly thanking K. C. for giving her husband back to her helped forge a lasting bond between their families.

In early 1997, K. C. was invited to the annual meeting of the Helicopter Association International, in southern California. Beck and Peach Weathers were also invited, and when they arrived at the airport in Anaheim, a helicopter identical to the one that rescued Beck was waiting to shuttle him from the airport to the convention center. At the banquet, he saw Madan K. C. for the first time since he had stepped from his helicopter, and they were both near tears. Madan was awarded the Robert E. Trimble Memorial Award, for distinguished service, and he received a standing ovation.

"Madan wasn't acting out of a desire for glory," Beck said. "Until the helicopter set down in Kathmandu, neither of us had any idea that anyone would be the least bit interested in the story."

In April 1997, another function was held at the Smithsonian Institution's National Air and Space Museum, and Beck was selected to present Madan the Aviation Week & Space Technology Laureate Award. In Kathmandu, K. C. was also awarded Nepal's highest honor, the Star of Nepal medal,

In 1963, after accomplishing a rare traverse of Everest, Willi Unsoeld had to be carried by Sherpas to a helicopter.

presented by His Majesty the King. "It was not really bravery," the charismatic K. C. said with humility. "It was in the line of duty."

"Through hard work, good judgment, and a fair amount of luck, we prevailed," Brad Ohlund reflected. "But not without a stiff reminder of the delicate place man occupies in nature. As for my own involvement, though I never went above Base Camp, I felt privileged, challenged, and humbled."

Filmmaker Greg MacGillivray was upbeat. "We are all proud of the team, and of their determination, courage, skill, and good judgment. Not only did they reach the summit, they had the patience to do it safely."

"Life in the mountains draws out the character of those that journey there," Dr. Jim Litch said. "Maybe this is one of the many reasons why we climb—to see ourselves at the core, not packaged and contained as we are when living within the constraints of technology and consumerism."

"Mountains are hazardous and there will be deaths," Dr. Tom Hornbein concluded, "and as the crowding increases, it's like setting up more pins at the end of the bowling alley: There are more to knock down."

Beck Weathers is sorry that he went to Everest, and he quietly admits, as if ashamed of his former ignorance, that what he was searching for was with him all along: home, health, family, and friends. But like others who have touched Everest's icy skin, he may have come away with something found nowhere else. "One lure of Everest is that the decisions you make there are real, and difficult, and you have to live with them," he reflected. His eyes gleamed, almost as if the spirit of Chomolungma were drawing him back. "No doubt, there will continue to be more good men and women willing to gamble and lose for the privilege of being in one of the world's most rare, beautiful places."

Everest is a contradiction: Beautiful and changeful, inviting and ferocious, it continues to attract climbers to its slopes.

THE 1996 *EVEREST* FILM TEAM

THE *EVEREST* FILM EXPEDITION TEAM

David Breashears, Newton, Massachusetts, U.S.A., Expedition
Leader and Film Co-Director and Cinematographer
Robert Schauer, Graz, Austria, Assistant Cameraman
Ed Viesturs, Seattle, Washington, U.S.A., Deputy Leader
Jamling Tenzing Norgay, Darjiling, West Bengal, India,
Climbing Leader
Araceli Segarra, Catalonia, Spain, Climber
Sumiyo Tsuzuki, Tokyo, Japan, Climber

Base Camp Personnel

Stephen Judson, Co-Director, IMAX Creative Specialist
Brad Ohlund, U.S.A., Photographic and Technical Consultant
Paula Viesturs, U.S.A., Base Camp Manager
Elizabeth Cohen, U.S.A., Expedition Production Manager
Audrey Salkeld, U.K., Journalist

Sherpas

Wongchu Sherpa, Chyangba, Nepal, Sirdar
Lhakpa Dorje Sherpa, Chitregaun, Nepal, Climbing Sirdar

Nepali Climbing Sherpas

Jangbu Sherpa, Chyangba; **Muktu Lhakpa Sherpa,** Dingjing;
Thilen Sherpa, Dingjing; **Dorje Sherpa,** Hosing; **Durga Tamang,**
Deusa Bogal; **Karsang Namgyal Sherpa,** Thame; **Rinji Sherpa,**
Chyangba; **Ngima Tamang,** Gautala; **Ang Pasang Sherpa,** Thame;
Ngawang Yonden Sherpa, Pangboche; **Gombu Chhiri Sherpa,**
Chitre; **Lhakpa Gyalzen Sherpa,** Ghat; **Kame Sherpa,** Bakam;
Chhuldim Sherpa, Namche Bazar; **Nima Dorje Tamang,** Piringding;
Lhakpa Gyalje Sherpa, Chyangba; **Pasang Phutar Sherpa,** Gautala

Nepali Non-Climbing Sherpas

Chyangba Tamang, Singati Chhap; **Lhakpa Sherpa,** Kerung;
Ngima Sherpa, Chyangba; **Rinji Tamang,** Jantar Khani; **Phuri
Sherpa,** Tingla

MACGILLIVRAY FREEMAN FILMS PRODUCTION TEAM

Production Team

Greg MacGillivray, Co-Director and Producer
Stephen Judson, Co-Writer, Co-Director, Producer, and Editor
Tim Cahill, Co-Writer
Alec Lorimore, Producer
Kathy Burke Almon, Production Manager
Debbie Fogel, Production Controller

Book Production

Linda Marcopulos, Project Manager
Matthew Muller, Image (15/70) Reproduction Supervisor

Film Production/Distribution Team

**Janna Emmel, Teresa Ferriera, Bill Bennett, Myles Connolly,
Robert Walker, Alice Casbara, Bob Harman, Mike Lutz, Lori Rick**

Advisers to the 1996 Everest *Film Expedition*

Cynthia Beall, S. Idell Pyle Professor of Anthropology and Professor
of Anatomy, Case Western Reserve University
Roger Bilham, Professor of Geology, University of Colorado, Boulder
James F. Fisher, Professor of Anthropology and Director of Asian
Studies, Carleton College
Kip Hodges, Professor and Founding Director, School of Earth
& Space Exploration, Arizona State University
Charles S. Houston, M.D.
Peter Molnar, Professor and Fellow of the Cooperative Institute
for Research in Environmental Sciences (CIRES), University of
Colorado, Boulder
Audrey Salkeld, Historian, Author
Lhakpa Norbu Sherpa, Former Chief Warden, Sagarmatha
National Park
Bradford Washburn, Photographer; Science Specialist; Founding
Director of Museum of Science, Boston
Broughton Coburn, Writer

ACKNOWLEDGMENTS

It would not have been possible to write this book without the generous cooperation of the climbers, film team, Base Camp staff, and academic advisers of the 1996 *Everest* Film Expedition.

In particular, I am indebted to Greg MacGillivray, Alec Lorimore, Teresa Ferriera, Kathy Almon, Myles Connolly, and Matthew Muller of MacGillivray Freeman Films for their help, vision, patience, and generous support. I'd like to thank Linda Marcopulos especially for her unending enthusiasm, encouragement, and attention to detail—and Steve Judson for his careful and skilled attention to the manuscript.

I am grateful to David Breashears, Arcturus Motion Pictures, and National Geographic Society editors Kevin Mulroy and Charles Kogod for their patience and guidance.

To no lesser degree, I appreciate the unswerving help of Liesl Clark of *NOVA*, Audrey Salkeld, Howie Masters of ABC-TV,

Ken Kamler, M.D., Lou Kasischke, Terry Krundick and the staff of Teton County Library, Kevin Craig of National Geographic, Bob Rice of Bob Rice's Weather Window, and my wife Didi Thunder; they deserve special thanks.

Many others offered factual information, critical comments, and inspiration, including but not limited to Ian Alsop, Stan Armington, Pete Athans, Myra Badia, Christian Beckwith, Ellen Bernstein, and Encyclopedia Britannica, Inc., Brent Bishop, Todd Burleson, Brian Carson, Lisa Choegyal, Kate Churchhill, Jeanette Connolly, Kanak Mani Dixit, Jenny Dublin, Janna Emmel, Peter Hackett, M.D., Elizabeth Hawley, Thomas Hornbein, M.D., Thomas H. Jukes, Richard J. Kohn, Kevin Kowalchuk of the Imax Corporation, Paul LaChappelle, Wendy Lama, James Litch, M.D., Rick Mandahl, Dave Mencin, Wangchuk Mesto, Hemanta Raj Mishra, Bruce Morrison, Brad Ohlund, Brian Peniston,

Tom and Sue Piozet, Gil Roberts, M.D., David Shensted, Jeremy Schmidt, Robert Schoene, M.D., Klev Shoening, Pete Shoening, Ang Rita Sherpa, Mingma Sherpa, Phurba Soman Sherpa, Wongchu Sherpa and Peak Promotions, David Shlim, M.D., Erica Stone, Susy Struble, Norbu Tenzing, Barbara Thunder, Peach Weathers, Seaborn "Beck" Weathers, M.D., Brian Weirum, Jim Williams, and Jed Williamson. I apologize for missing others who also contributed selflessly to this broad-ranging effort. — B.C.

ABOUT THE AUTHOR

Broughton Coburn has spent more than half his life living and working in the Himalaya region. As a writer and speaker, he specializes in crafting narratives of the people and landscape of the Himalaya. His other books include *Nepali Aama: Life Lessons of a Himalayan Woman, Aama in America: A Pilgrimage of the Heart,* and, most recently, *The Vast Unknown: America's First Ascent of Everest.*

FURTHER READING

Anker, Conrad, and others. *The Call of Everest: The History, Science, and Future of the World's Tallest Mountain.* National Geographic Books, 2013.

Anker, Conrad, and David Roberts. *The Last Explorer: Finding Mallory on Mount Everest.* Simon & Schuster, 1999.

Bonnington, Chris. *Everest Expeditions Omnibus.* Weidenfeld & Nicolson, 2002.

Boukreev, Anatoli. *Above the Clouds: The Diaries of a High-Altitude Mountaineer.* St. Martin's Griffin, 2002.

Breashears, David. *High Exposure: An Enduring Passion for Everest and Unforgiving Places.* Simon & Schuster, 1999.

Breashears, David, and Audrey Salkeld. *Last Climb: The Legendary Everest Expeditions of George Mallory.* National Geographic, 1999.

Coburn, Broughton. *The Vast Unknown: The First American Ascent of Everest.* Random House, 2013.

Gilman, Peter, ed. *Everest: The Best Writing and Pictures from Seventy Years of Human Endeavor.* Little, Brown and Company, 1993.

Groom, Michael. *Sheer Will.* Random House, 2000.

Hornbein, Thomas. *Everest: The West Ridge.* Mountaineers Books, 1998.

Kasischke, Lou. *After the Wind: 1996 Everest Tragedy, One Survivor's Story.* Good Hart Publishing, 2014.

Krakauer, Jon. *Into Thin Air: A Personal Account of the Mount Everest Disaster.* Villard Books, 1997.

Messner, Reinhold. *All Fourteen 8,000ers.* Mountaineers Books, 1999.

Norgay, Jamling Tenzing. *Touching My Father's Soul: A Sherpa's Journey to the Top of Everest.* HarperSanFrancisco, 2000.

Viesturs, Ed, and David Roberts. *The Mountain: My Time on Everest.* Random House, 2013.

———. *No Shortcuts to the Top: Climbing the World's 14 Highest Peaks.* Random House, 2009.

Weathers, Beck. *Left for Dead: My Journey Home From Everest.* Villard, 2000.

Whittaker, Jim. *A Life on the Edge.* Mountaineers Books, 1999.

CREDITS

ILLUSTRATIONS CREDITS

Cover, Neal Beidleman; 2-3, Grant Dixon/Hedgehog House New Zealand; 5, The Asahi Shimbun Premium/Getty Images; 6, David Breashears/MacGillivray Freeman Films; 8, Cory Richards/National Geographic Creative; 9, Cory Richards/National Geographic Creative; 10-11, Cory Richards/National Geographic Creative; 12 (UP), Bogdan Jankowski; 12 (LOLE), Mallory and Irvine Expedition/Jim Fagiolo/Getty Images; 12 (LORT), GOMBU, NAWANG/National Geographic Creative; 12-13, Anton Rogozin/Shutterstock; 13 (UPLE), Stephen Venables; 13 (UPRT), Simone Moro; 13 (LOLE), Neal Beidleman; 13 (LORT), Prakash Mathema/AFP/Getty Images; 14, Scott Fischer, courtesy Jeannie Price; 16, Andy Bardon Photography; 17, Jonathan Irish/National Geographic Creative; 18, Grant Dixon/Hedgehog House/Minden Pictures/National Geographic Creative; 21, Sumiyo Tsuzuki/MacGillivray Freeman Films; 23, Ed Viesturs; 24-5, Pete Ryan/National Geographic Creative; 26, HO/Reuters/Corbis; 27, David Breashears/MacGillivray Freeman Films; 28, Barry Bishop/National Geographic Creative; 29, MacGillivray Freeman Films; 30, Andy Bardon Photography; 32, Gavin Hellier/Getty Images; 33, Sisse Brimberg and Cotton Coulson/National Geographic Creative; 34, AWL Images/Getty Images; 35, Edmund Hillary/Royal Geographical Society; 36-7, David Breashears/MacGillivray Freeman Films; 38, Robert Schauer/MacGillivray Freeman Films; 39, Richard I'Anson/Getty Images; 40, Pete Ryan/National Geographic Creative; 41, Anne B. Keiser/National Geographic Creative; 44, Grant Dixon/Getty Images; 45, William Thompson; 46-7, Natalia Maroz/Shutterstock; 48, Robb Kendrick Photography; 49, Ethan Welty/TandemStock.com; 50-51, Steele Burrow/TandemStock.com; 52, Dmitri Alexander/National Geographic Creative; 54-5, David Breashears/MacGillivray Freeman Films; 56, Robb Kendrick Photography; 57, Robb Kendrick Photography; 59, Broughton Coburn; 60, fotoVoyager/Getty Images; 62, Richard I'Anson/Getty Images; 63, Robb Kendrick/Aurora Photos; 64, Ethan Welty/TandemStock.com; 66, Colin Monteath/Minden Pictures/National Geographic Creative; 67, Ethan Welty/TandemStock.com; 68-9, Tim Watson/National Geographic Your Shot; 71, Gordon Wiltsie; 73, Barry Bishop/National Geographic Creative; 74-5, David Breashears/MacGillivray Freeman Films; 76, Alex Treadway/Getty Images; 79, Andy Bardon Photography; 82, Araceli Segarra/MacGillivray Freeman Films; 83, Alfred Gregory/Royal Geographical Society; 85, Robert Schauer/MacGillivray Freeman Films; 86-7, © Eddie Bauer. Photo by Jake Norton; 88, Werner Van Steen/Getty Images; 89, AP Photo/Mountain Madness; 91, Aaron Huey/National Geographic Creative;

92, Sumiyo Tsuzuki/MacGillivray Freeman Films; 94-5, David Breashears/MacGillivray Freeman Films; 96, © 2012 Mayo Foundation for Medical Education and Research; used with permission; 97, Stephen Venables; 98, Aaron Huey/National Geographic Creative; 99, Cory Richards/National Geographic Creative; 100-1, Sumiyo Tsuzuki/MacGillivray Freeman Films; 102, Bobby Model/National Geographic Creative; 103, Cory Richards/National Geographic Creative; 104, Araceli Segarra/MacGillivray Freeman Films; 107, Barry Bishop/National Geographic Creative; 108, Alfred Gregory/Royal Geographical Society; 109, Luther Jerstad/NGS Archives; 110-11, David Breashears/MacGillivray Freeman Films; 112-13, Daniel Prudek/Shutterstock; 114, Andy Bardon Photography; 116, Danny Xu/Shutterstock; 117, Andy Bardon Photography; 118, Robert Schauer/MacGillivray Freeman Films; 119, David Breashears/MacGillivray Freeman Films; 120-21, David Breashears/MacGillivray Freeman Films; 122, David Breashears/MacGillivray Freeman Films; 123, NASA; 124-5, Andy Bardon Photography; 127, Andy Bardon/National Geographic Creative; 128, Andy Bardon Photography; 129, David Breashears/MacGillivray Freeman Films; 130, AFP/Stringer/Getty Images; 131, Andy Bardon/National Geographic Creative; 132, Max Lowe; 133, Simone Moro; 134-5, Robert Schauer/MacGillivray Freeman Films; 136, Robert Schauer/MacGillivray Freeman Films; 139, Anton Sokolov/iStockphoto; 141, Neal Beidleman; 142-3, Neal Beidleman 144, Robert Schauer/MacGillivray Freeman Films; 145, Stefen Chow/Aurora Photos/Corbis; 146, Garrett Madison; 147, Robert Schauer/MacGillivray Freeman Films; 148, Pete McBride/National Geographic Creative; 149, Robert Schauer/MacGillivray Freeman Films; 150, Ganesh Thakuri/Utmost Adventure Trekking; 151, Scott Fischer, courtesy Jeannie Price; 152, William F. Unsoeld; 154, Robert Schauer/MacGillivray Freeman Films; 155, Dr. Ken Kamler; 156, Araceli Segarra/MacGillivray Freeman Films; 157, Colin Monteath/Minden Pictures/National Geographic Creative; 158-9, Araceli Segarra/MacGillivray Freeman Films; 160, Robert Schauer/MacGillivray Freeman Films; 161, Alex Treadway/National Geographic Creative; 162, Gopal Chitrakar/Reuters/Corbis; 163, Fredrik Schenholm/National Geographic My Shot; 164, Neal Beidleman; 167, Robert Schauer/MacGillivray Freeman Films; 168, Kristoffer Erickson; 169, Nawang Sherpa/Bogati/ZUMA/Corbis; 170-71, Kiwisoul/Shutterstock; 172, Kristoffer Erickson; 173, Barry Bishop/National Geographic Creative; 174-5, Reinhold Messner; 176, Nena Holguin; 178-9, Tommy Heinrich; 182, David Breashears/MacGillivray Freeman Films; 183, David Breashears/MacGillivray Freeman Films; 185, Robert Schauer/MacGillivray Freeman Films; 186-7, Barry Bishop/National Geographic Creative; 188, Wally Berg; 190-91, Robert Schauer/MacGillivray Freeman Films; 192-3, Robert Schauer/MacGillivray Freeman Films; 194, Robert Schauer/MacGillivray Freeman Films; 196, Barry Bishop/National Geographic Creative; 197, Robert Schauer/MacGillivray Freeman Films; 199, Ed Webster/mtnimagery.com; 200-201, Robert Schauer/MacGillivray Freeman Films; 202, David Breashears/MacGillivray Freeman Films; 203, Jamling Norgay/MacGillivray Freeman Films; 204, Ed Webster/mtnimagery.com; 205, Andy Bardon Photography; 207, Araceli Segarra/MacGillivray Freeman Films; 208, Ed Viesturs/MacGillivray Freeman Films; 209, REUTERS/Picture Norgay Archive; 210-11, Robert Schauer/MacGillivray Freeman Films; 212, David Breashears; 213, Rob Howard/Corbis; 214, David Breashears/MacGillivray Freeman Films; 215, David L. Dingman; 216-17, Kiwisoul/Shutterstock; Back Cover, David Breashears/MacGillivray Freeman Films.

MAP/GRAPHICS CREDITS

42–43, 65, 80–81: Coburn, Broughton. *Everest: Mountain Without Mercy.* National Geographic Society: 1997.
27, 84, 180, 212: Salisbury, Richard, and Elizabeth Hawley. *The Himalayan Database.* American Alpine Club: 2014.

TEXT CREDITS

9, Viesturs, edviesturs.com/about-ed; 16, Krakauer, *Into Thin Air,* Knopf/Doubleday (Random House), 1997. This quotation and others used by permission from the publisher; 20, Hunt, www.mnteverest.net/quote.html; 22, Ullman, *Americans on Everest,* J. B. Lippincott & Co., 1964; 27, Dyhrenfurth, American Alpine Club, explore.americanalpineclub.org/index.php/Detail/Object/Show/object_id/1336; 31, Weathers, *Storm Over Everest,* PBS, 2008; 40, Kohnì and Rimpoche, *Everest: Mountain Without Mercy,* 1997; 45, Jenkins, ngm.national-geographic.com/2013/06/125-everest-maxed-out/jenkins-text; 48, Muir, 1896; 56, Krakauer, *Into Thin Air,* Knopf/Doubleday (Random House), 1997; 58, Messner, *Mountains From Space: Peaks and Ranges of the Seven Continents,* Abrams, 2005; 61, Davis; Huw Lewis-Jones, *Mountain Heroes: Portraits of Adventure,* Conway Maritime Press, 2011. This quotation and others used by permission from the publisher; 66, Cool; Huw Lewis-Jones, *Mountain Heroes: Portraits of Adventure,* Conway Maritime Press, 2011; 70, Beidleman, *Storm Over Everest,* PBS, 2008; 72, Messner, *All Fourteen 8,000ers,* Mountaineers Books, 1999; 78, Kasischke, *Storm Over Everest,* PBS, 2008; 83, Morton, *National Geographic Adventure,* adventure.nationalgeographic.com/adventure/everest/everest-at-50-cory-richards/; 84, Researcher at the Institute of Personality Assessment and Research; Coburn, *The Vast Unknown,* Crown, 2013; 89, Mallory; Huw Lewis-Jones, *Mountain Heroes: Portraits of Adventure,* Conway Maritime Press, 2011; 90, Dyhrenfurth; Richards, *National Geographic Adventure,* adventure.nationalgeographic.com/adventure/everest/everest-at-50-cory-richards/; 93, Groom, www.mnteverest.net/quote.html; 98, Anker, *National Geographic Adventure,* adventure.nationalgeographic.com/adventure/everest/everest-at-50-cory-richards/; 102, Weihenmayer; Huw Lewis-Jones, *Mountain Heroes: Portraits of Adventure,* Conway Maritime Press, 2011; 106, Krakauer, *Into Thin Air,* Knopf/Doubleday (Random House), 1997; 108, Hillary, *Voices From the Summit,* National Geographic, 2000; 115, Scott, *Voices From the Summit,* National Geographic, 2000; 123, Krakauer, *Into Thin Air,* Knopf/Doubleday (Random House), 1997; 126, Viesturs, *No Shortcuts to the Top,* Broadway Books, 2006; 138, Mallory, from Julie Summers, *Fearless on Everest: The Quest for Sandy Irvine;* 140, Wetzle, *Outside,* 2006; 145, Messner, *The Crystal Horizon: Everest—The First Solo Ascent,* Mountaineers Books, 1989; 148, Norton, *National Geographic Adventure,* adventure.nationalgeographic.com/adventure/everest/everest-at-50-cory-richards/; 150, Jerstad; McCallum, *Everest Diary,* Follett, 1966; 153, Breashears, *The Call of Everest,* National Geographic, 2013; 157, Houston; Houston, *Going Higher,* American Alpine Clib, 1980; 162, Burns, *New York Times,* 1996; 166, Odell, *Everest: Mountain Without Mercy,* 1997; 177, Bishop, *National Geographic,* 1963; 181, Houston; *Voices From the Summit,* National Geographic, 2000; 184, Hornbein, *Everest: The West Ridge,* Mountaineers Books, 1998; 195, Messner; Rice, *Guardian,* 2004 observer.theguardian.com/osm/story/0,,1315445,00.html; 198, Bishop, *National Geographic,* 1963; 203, Hillary, *Voices From the Summit,* National Geographic, 2000; 204, Norgay, mnteverest.net/quote.html; 206, Meyer, *Rocky Mountain News,* 1996; 209, Hillary, *New York Times,* 1996; 214, Clinch; Coburn, *The Vast Unknown,* Crown, 2013.

INDEX

EVEREST
Broughton Coburn

PUBLISHED BY THE NATIONAL GEOGRAPHIC SOCIETY

Gary E. Knell, *President and Chief Executive Officer*
John M. Fahey, *Chairman of the Board*
Declan Moore, *Chief Media Officer*
Chris Johns, *Chief Content Officer*

PREPARED BY THE BOOK DIVISION

Hector Sierra, *Senior Vice President and General Manager*
Lisa Thomas, *Senior Vice President and Editorial Director*
Jonathan Halling, *Creative Director*
Marianne R. Koszorus, *Design Director*
Susan Tyler Hitchcock, *Senior Editor*
R. Gary Colbert, *Production Director*
Jennifer A. Thornton, *Director of Managing Editorial*
Susan S. Blair, *Director of Photography*
Meredith C. Wilcox, *Director, Administration and Rights Clearance*

STAFF FOR THIS BOOK

Kate J. Armstrong, *Editor*
Elisa Gibson, *Art Director*
Matt Propert, *Illustrations Editor*
Linda Makarov, *Designer*
Lori Rick, *MacGillivray Freeman Films Liaison*
Carl Mehler, *Director of Maps*
Juan José Valdés, *The Geographer*
Martin Gamache, *Senior Graphics Editor*
Matthew W. Chwastyk, Michael McNey, *Map Production*
Marshall Kiker, *Associate Managing Editor*
Judith Klein, *Senior Production Editor*
Will Cline, *Production Manager*
Constance Roellig, *Rights Clearance Specialist*
Katie Olsen, *Design Production Specialist*
Nicole Miller, *Design Production Assistant*
Bobby Barr, *Manager, Production Services*
John Chow, *Imaging*

The Library of Congress has cataloged the 1997 edition as follows:
Coburn, Broughton, 1951-
    Everest : mountain without mercy / by Broughton Coburn;
introduction by Tim Cahill, afterword by David Breashears.
        p.   cm.
    Includes index.
    ISBN 0-7922-7014-2
    1. Mount Everest Expedition (1996) 2. Mount Everest
Expedition
    (1996)—Pictorial works. 3. Mountaineering accidents—Everest,
    Mount (China and Nepal) 4. Mountaineering accidents—Everest,
Mount
    (China and Nepal)—Pictorial works. 5. IMAX Corporation.
    I. Title.
    GV199.44.E85C63 1997
    796.5'22'095496—dc21
97-10765

For more information, please call 1-800-NGS LINE (647-5463) or write to the following address:

National Geographic Society
1145 17th Street NW
Washington, D.C. 20036-4688 U.S.A.

Your purchase supports our nonprofit work and makes you part of our global community. Thank you for sharing our belief in the power of science, exploration and storytelling to change the world. To activate your member benefits, complete your free membership profile at natgeo.com/joinnow.

For information about special discounts for bulk purchases, please contact National Geographic Books Special Sales: ngspecsales@ngs.org

For rights or permissions inquiries, please contact National Geographic Books Subsidiary Rights: ngbookrights@ngs.org

ISBN: 978-1-4262-1585-8

Printed in the United States of America

15/CK-CML/1

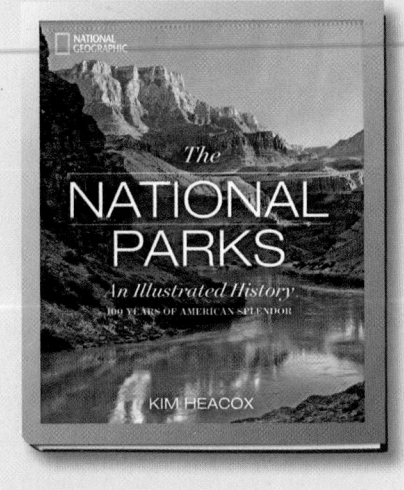

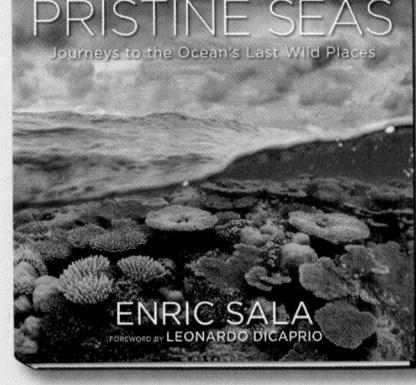
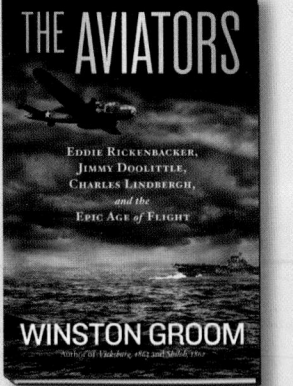
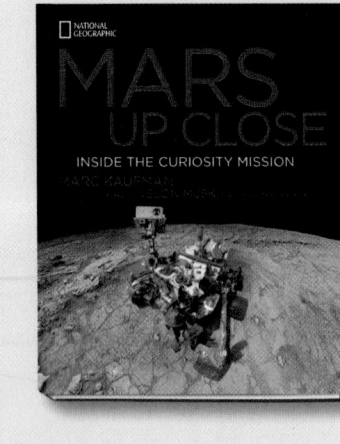